# The Peninsular War with the Coldstream Guards

# The Peninsular War with the Coldstream Guards

Reminiscences of an officer
in Portugal and Spain

John Cowell Stepney

LEONAUR

*The Peninsular War with
the Coldstream Guards'
Reminiscences of an officer
in Portugal and Spain*
by John Cowell Stepney

First published under the title
*Leaves From the Diary
of an Officer of the Guards*

Leonaur is an imprint
of Oakpast Ltd

ISBN: 978-1-84677-926-8 (hardcover)
ISBN: 978-1-84677-925-1 (softcover)

**http://www.leonaur.com**

Publisher's Notes

In the interests of authenticity, the spellings, grammar and place names used have been retained from the original editions.

The opinions of the authors represent a view of events in which he was a participant related from his own perspective, as such the text is relevant as an historical document.

The views expressed in this book are not necessarily those of the publisher.

# Contents

# Contents

To Major-General Henry Bentinck,
the Officers, Non-Commissioned Officers,
and Soldiers of the Brigade of Guards,
Serving With Lord Raglan's Army in the Crimea,
These Reminiscences of Past Services
With the Brigade are Inscribed
With Fervent Attachment to Their Colours
by
A Veteran Comrade.

# Preface

These papers, taken from the *Diary of an Officer of the Guards*, having appeared in a periodical and met with approbation, are now, for the first time, offered to the public in a collective form. They are trifles, but truthful ones. In dedicating them to the brigade to which the author once belonged, he cannot but remember how few remain of those who stood in its ranks when he left them:

*Hæc data pœna diu viventibus.*

Yet, as some of his proudest and most joyous days were passed in their ranks, he is tempted to address his recollections of former days to the present maintainers of their Sovereign's power and their country's glory.

*Nulli Secundus*

is the well-known motto of one of their regiments. That all of them would maintain it intact, and add fresh laurels to those won by their gallant forefathers, was undoubted. Their recent splendid achievement on the heights of the Alma is the proof.

London, October 10, 1854.

## CHAPTER 1

# Departure From England

In May, 1809, I was gazetted as an ensign in the —— Regiment, and in July of the following year was ordered to join a detachment of the Guards destined for our first battalion then serving with Lord Wellington's army in Portugal. Every hour of my home duties was looked upon as tedious until the longed-for moment for joining my regiment on active service should arrive. Having obtained a short leave of absence, to bid my friends adieu, I joined a draft or detachment of two hundred men and eight officers, under command of Lieutenant Colonel S——, at Kingston-on-Thames, and the next day we proceeded on our march to Portsmouth.

On the 29th, to the tune of a militia band, accompanied by the cheers of the town's-people, we marched down to the sally-port, and embarked in smacks, to be conveyed to Spithead, where our ship lay. This was a vessel of 300 tons burden, called the *Lord Eldon*—an old creaky craft, by origin a collier, by transmutation a transport, remarkable for the narrowness of its capacity and the slowness of its motions. Although considered to be sound, experience betrayed its frequent leaky propensities.

Many now living remember the employment of such an old vessel by the State. Human genius has since applied a power to drive ships against adverse winds and mountainous seas, to roll carriages at the rate of fifty miles an hour over the surface of the earth, and, annihilating time and space, to chain by its electric spark the lightning of heaven, to waft man's wishes "from Indus to the Pole."

The conveyance of troops on board transports in those days was anything but luxurious, rapid, or even safe. After a month's tugging at our anchor, and bobbing up and down at Spithead, where contrary winds and foul weather detained us, at last on the 31st August, 1810, we weighed anchor, by signal from our Commodore Captain Mackenzie Eraser, of the *Undaunted* frigate, and dropped down off Yarmouth in the Isle of Wight.

On the following day (1st September), under convoy of the frigate and five brigs of war, 130 sail of transports and merchantmen passed through the Needles and lay down Channel with a leading wind. Foul weather and adverse winds soon again beset us, and we took six days beating to windward before we reached the chops of the Channel and came off Falmouth.

Although we had all started in the highest spirits, our imaginations were sobered by bad weather and boisterous seas; realities are very unsentimental, and sea-sickness is a sad undignified disorder. The weather however now became calm, and the wind light though fair; we began to get our sea legs and recover our appetites. A boat was lowered and sent on shore for fresh provisions; on its return towards evening, the breeze freshening, we made sail again, and took leave of our country, as the setting sun lingered over and lighted up the fast fading shores, bays, and hills of our dear native land, and then we stretched away toward the blue waters of the Bay of Biscay. A fresh and favourable breeze throughout the night enabled us to run down nearly a hundred miles, when morning showed us the French coast off Cape Ushant. The wind still freshened, and we continued our course directly across the Bay.

For a couple of days it blew very hard, and the *Lord Eldon* (as usual) sprang a leak. Our men pumped cheerfully and manfully night and day, our officers sharing with the men spell and spell about. The leak relieved us from the smell of bilge-water; a dead calm succeeded, and we lay like a log rolling to and fro in a tremendous swell; as the old song has it—

*There she lay*

*All the day*
*In the Bay*
*Of Biscay oh.*

The sea was like glass; every board of our old brig creaked like the shoes of its namesake, and the canvas flapped round the masts in helpless idleness, whilst we were exposed to a burning sun on deck and to stifling heat below. Our impatience to advance seemed to increase in proportion to our inability to move. Next the measles broke out among our men, and did not spare the officers; two hundred privates and ten of us were crammed into a space not sufficient to contain half the number. Our captain, who much more frequently had a glass at his mouth than one at his eye, had never extended his maritime knowledge beyond a voyage with coals from Shields to London and back again, and was perfectly innocent of ever taking an observation. He was a red-faced, gooseberry-eyed, drunken Northumbrian skipper; and his vessel, the *ci-devant* collier, an ugly, slow, and leaky drowning machine, always going to leeward like a haystack.

From the various accounts that reached us previous to our sailing, our people were expected to be in movement before we joined them, and we feared the delay would, as it did eventually, prevent us from sharing in a general action with the enemy. At length a favourable wind sprang up, and the first symptom we had of nearing the land of our future operations was coming in sight of the Berlengas rocks.

The practice of sailing under convoy in time of war, with so near a neighbour as France for an enemy, was lying to every evening, for the heavy sailing vessels of the fleet to come up and the convoy to be well together during the night, for fear of the enemy's cruisers cutting off any straggling vessels. This was annoying to the head-most ships, that were leading with a favourable gale, and here again we lost way. I know not whether in this circumstance originated my disgust for travelling in slow company, but ever since I certainly have strenuously avoided "slow coaches."

One still moonlight night, as we ran down the coast of Portugal, we heard what we fancied to be the distant roll of cannon from the shore. After listening with mute attention, we ventured to communicate our hopes and fears to each other, and to a grim old sailor who was standing silently on the forecastle. On being applied to for his opinion, he rejoined, with a tug at his waistband, a twirl of his quid, and a turn on his heel, "It's the breakers on the shore." This dry correction of our innocent inexperience was highly relished by us.

On the 14th we came within sight of the rock of Lisbon. A Portuguese pilot came on board: he was unlike any of his breed in our own country, and we gazed on his dress, his mahogany-coloured countenance and Jew-like profile, with curiosity. We neared the coast, but, the wind failing, we did not enter the Tagus till the evening of the next day. Few, except such as have been some weeks at sea, can conceive the satisfaction of approaching land; but still fewer, without having experienced it, could enter into our feelings, as we passed up the Tagus in a fine summer evening of the month of September. The gardens in their richest foliage, the scent from the shore of the aromatic productions of the South, the lovely coast, the magic beauty of Lisbon, its white mansions, convents, cupolas, palaces and churches, reflected in the blue waters of the Tagus, appeared like fairyland to us. All was new, both earth and sky; and most of us were at that age when impressions such as these are perhaps the strongest; we seemed as if we had fallen into another world. Our errand also, that of supporting our country's honour in arms, had its proud share in these pleasurable sensations.

It was dusk before we let drop our anchor off Belem. An order from our commanding officer forbade our going on shore for that night. Under pretence however of getting a supply of vegetables and fruit, we manned a boat and landed on the side of the river opposite to Lisbon, where we obtained an abundance of fine grapes and fruit of all kinds, with some delicious wine. The state of our own country, which, from its long protracted wars against nearly all Europe, had excluded a free intercourse with foreigners, rendered all we saw of them doubly strange; their habits, manners, appearance, all were unlike our own, and this was the first time I had ever set foot on a foreign strand.

The next day (the 16th) a portion of the officers were allowed to go on shore, and I was among the number. On landing I must confess the illusions of the previous evening were nearly dispelled, with regard to the lovely city we had viewed from afar: each step we advanced, filth in the greatest quantity and of the most disgusting nature presented itself, accompanied by a corresponding stench; and the strange figures, the uncouth noises, the appearance of representatives of every country in their national dress, from Christian to Turk, congregated in one dense crowd, was fairly bewildering.

Attention was no sooner attracted by one strange costume, than another still more curious diverted us, and so on in succession; till our sensations, agog as they were for novelty, required a double portion of the usual faculties, visual and auricular, to see and comprehend what passed before us. In addition to all this, on a nearer view I found one half the town consisted of ruins, from the great earthquake of half a century ago; the remaining mansions appeared but thinly inhabited, except by English officers and *employés,* and the gayest part of Lisbon was occupied by mercantile houses and shops.

We arrived at the inn, a dirty, spacious, dear, and badly attended hotel, with good wine and good living, as *we* thought at least, who had just quitted a transport. On landing, we went to report our arrival to the Commandant, Colonel Peacock, of the Guards[1], who asked us all to dine with him the next day. Mr. Stuart[2], our minister, gave a ball, to which we were also invited. Neither "love nor money" however could procure me a bed at the inn that night; all were filled; some by officers who had come down on leave from the army, others by those either embarking, or, like ourselves, disembarking ; the squadron of our navy in the Tagus also took their share of the inns when they

---

1. Afterwards Lieut. General Sir Warren Peacock, K.C.B.
2. Afterwards Lord Stuart de Rothsay, our Ambassador at Paris.

came on shore.

Our men being still on board the transport, we were not entitled to billets; I contrived at last, through a brother officer who had just left the army, to obtain a bed in the apartments of a friend of his, the superior of a monastery. The goodly monk, who bestowed upon me a lodging, was a lively comfortable-sized *clerico*, who, according to his own account, had dreamed of more things in his philosophy than saying his prayers; and he spoke of the world, and what was passing in it, as one who was on good terms both with it and himself.

In the evening we attended our dinner and ball; the latter was very gay: the military and naval uniforms of our own country mingled with those of Portugal and Spain; the dark eyes and expressive countenances of the Lisbon ladies, contrasted with the fair faces of our countrywomen, formed a novel-and agreeable mixture. The women of Portugal have fine eyes, which are their principal attraction, and more expressive countenances than the tamer beauties of the North; but their skin is generally sallow, and neither in clearness of complexion nor regularity of feature can they vie with their neighbours the Spaniards or the natives of Italy. With respect to the Portuguese men, they are generally a Jewish-looking race, and in the higher orders there prevails a diminutiveness of stature which is anything but dignified.

The hospitable entertainment and affability of our minister were well known and appreciated by the whole of the British Army during this eventful period. At this ball we heard that intelligence had been received, that Marshal Massena with 120,000 men had taken Ciudad Rodrigo, and advanced; and a sharp affair near Almeida, on the Coa, had taken place between our Light Division under Craufurd and the advance-guard of the French army; that Massena was about to invade Portugal, and that our army was already in movement, We had it also intimated to us from the commandant, that we were to shift our transports to others, and go by sea round to Mondego Bay.

On our way from this gay scene, conning over the new order of our destination, we encountered an army of half-wild dogs in the streets. These animals, in conjunction with pigs, were the sole scavengers of Lisbon; and as night approached, the canine dustmen came forth from their dens in the ruins of the town, to feed on its filth, and fight over it half the night through. Sometimes even they were bold enough, if interrupted at their orgies, to attack foot-passengers. They were not destroyed, in consequence of the sanitary service they rendered to his Majesty of Portugal's capital.

On the 18th, after taking leave of my comely landlord, who treated me with much kindness and hospitality, and who in very good English gave me a general invitation to come and lodge at his convent whenever I returned to Lisbon, I hastened on board. The best part of two days was now occupied in shipping and unshipping, and laying in a little stock of provisions, to carry us on our new excursion. My lot, together with that of the colonel, a captain, with one other sub. and a hundred men, fell to the good ship *N. K transport*; and on the 21st of September, in company with three other vessels containing detachments of other regiments, we left the Tagus with a fair wind.

At Mondego Bay the forces under Sir Arthur Wellesley had landed in 1808, previously to the battles of Vimeira and Rolica and the Convention of Cintra. The object of sending us round by sea was to save time and fatigue to our men, and to disembark nearer to our army. The wind how. ever proved most unfavourable, and we were seven days at sea, performing a distance of twenty leagues. Supposing we should accomplish our voyage in forty-eight hours at most, the provisions were insufficient, and we were necessarily placed on very short commons; the day we arrived, the whole of our sea stock, ship's allowance and all, being consumed.

We landed on the 28th at Buarcos, near Figueiras, a small fishing-village on the north side of the bay; we reached the shore from our transport in uncouth Portuguese boats and in a tremendous surf. One of our men, Chissel by name, was lost in the operation of landing; the boat was overcrowded, and the poor fellow sat on the gunnel; a rolling ground-swell sea struck us as we neared the beach and pitched him overboard. He was a swimmer, but the weight of his knapsack sank him, to rise no more. Here we heard rumours of our army having been sharply engaged with the French under Massena, who had advanced into Portugal with 100,000 men.

At Figueiras, as soon as our men were billeted, I went to seek my quarters, and, not speaking a word of Portuguese, met with some difficulty. At last I found myself lodged in an onion-loft, together with an Irish hospital mate, the purest piece of unsophisticated potato I ever beheld, with red hair, original ideas, and a splendid brogue. I was simple enough to believe that this was "roughing it!"—four campaigns in the Peninsula convinced me to the contrary; and on many a rainy and house-less night I looked back to my onion-loft with regret.

The next morning (29th) five hundred of us, detachments of different regiments, amongst whom were some of the 95th Rifles under Captain Beckwith[3], had three days' rations served out, and we left Figueiras to march to Montemor-o-Velho, a small pretty village in the Val de Mondego. The river Mondego rises in the mountains of the Serra d'Estrella, near Guarda, takes its course through the province of Beira, and waters a most lovely valley, to which it gives its name; after passing the towns of Celerico and Coimbra, it debouches into the sea at Figueiras. Before the rains set in, it is fordable almost everywhere.

On our arrival at Montemor, we were scarcely settled in our quarters, when we distinctly heard a cannonade,—no "breakers on the shore" this time! our island ears were now first saluted by the sound of hostile shot. On the 30th, by daylight, we were on our march to Coimbra, and had proceeded about ten miles, when we encountered the sick and wounded, with baggage and stores, proceeding in boats down the river to embark for Lisbon, and were informed by them that our army, in an action on the 27th, had repulsed the enemy with severe loss, and that the Portuguese troops who shared in the engagement had greatly

---

3. This officer, after serving with great credit to himself through the Peninsular campaigns, reached the rank of colonel, and is a C.B. He lost his leg at Waterloo.

distinguished themselves.

Our forces however were in full retreat for Lisbon. After about an hour's more marching, we perceived at a distance on our left some small bodies of cavalry slowly descending a mountain; our telescopes were immediately put in requisition, and enabled us to discover them to be some of the French advanced posts. There was not amongst us a single round of ball-cartridge, none having been served out to us on landing. A staff-officer at this moment rode up, and said all our army had passed to the left bank of the river, and that our brigade was, to our agreeable surprise, at a village not far distant from us on the opposite side.

We consequently forded the stream up to our waists, and in an hour after joined our battalion at a place called San Martinho do Bispo, within a mile of Coimbra on the road to Lisbon. San Martinho, for a Portuguese hamlet, was well looking, prettily situated, and thriving,—the Bispo no doubt deriving profit therefrom. After delivering over the detachment of our men to the commanding officers of the regiments which formed our brigade, and the officers being posted to the different companies of our battalions, our next step on joining our corps was making the acquaintance of those of our future comrades to whom we were as yet unknown.

Amongst them I remember well being struck by the appearance of an intellectual-looking, high-spirited, laughing little fellow, agreeably lounging in a many-coloured bed-gown out of a cottage window in the main thoroughfare of our village. He seemed to stand in high popular estimation, and was warmly greeted by all who passed. Poor W——! I here first made his acquaintance, from which an intimacy and friendship resulted, that lasted forty years and ended only with his life.

Our brigade, after a night's march from the Serra de Busaco, had reached the village only in the morning of the day we joined them. B——, my brother Sub., belonged to the company to which I was attached. We were quartered together, and after the evening's refreshment, such as it was, we partook of the same mattress, laid on the mud floor of our cabin, sleeping in our clothes and in our cloaks, divesting our feet only of our boots. This was a new situation; a wakeful night ensued, and I had ample time to ponder on the starry sky through the glassless and shutterless window. My more veteran comrade however slept soundly.

We were now within, a short distance of the French Army, whose name and exploits had carried terror throughout Europe. The following morning, long before it was light, we were roused from our lowly sleeping-berth by bugle and drum, and sallied forth. The stars shone brightly; we hurried to our alarm post, and marched to an olive grove outside the village. The animated scene, being the first of the kind I had witnessed, was both interesting and stirring. The well-bronzed features and muscular forms of our soldiers and new comrades, the light way in which they spoke of fatigue, privation, and danger, the hearty laugh, loud and long, and the careless indifference of what the morrow might bring, indicated the right stuff for soldiers; such men were not easily overcome, and, even if worsted by overwhelming numbers, would afford an enemy no cheaply-bought victory.

# CHAPTER 2

# End of 1810 Campaign

The division to which my regiment belonged, amounting to nearly 7,000 men, were receiving rations: the busy hum of so many voices, the glare from the bivouac fires glancing on the arms, accoutrements, and hard visages of the men, the dark olive foliage overhanging this picture of apparent confusion, struck most forcibly upon the eye of a novice. Soon, however, one roll of the drum silenced all the busy noise; we stood to our arms, and a bayonet might be heard to fall. The column moved slowly off; daylight discovered our whole army in full retreat along parallel roads.

The unpractised eye, unaccustomed to view large masses, would estimate the columns, as seen in loose marching order, at double their real force, from the extent of ground they covered. For miles, over hill and dale, through heath and wood, clouds of dust betrayed their direction and line of movement; and even amidst the dark pine-forests, the masses were to be detected by the glancing of the sun upon their arms, which, according to Horse-Guards' regulations, it was thought necessary to keep as bright as the brass knocker of a suburban villa.

New as this was to the uninitiated, it was nothing in comparison to the accompanying flight of the entire Portuguese nation. It was a fearful sight to behold a whole nation's panic. It looked as though no soul that could move had remained behind. The strong, the healthy, and the young were in arms; the old, the decrepit, delicate women and young children, were on foot in flight, wandering through forest, heath, and mountain— in by-paths and cross-roads—over the face of their own fatherland, to avoid the destroyer.

They carried on donkeys and mules, in their arms and on their heads, all of their small worldly chattels they could convey; the rest was buried or destroyed, and nothing was left to their foe but bare walls and empty habitations. The French might revel in a wilderness of dwellings—they were indeed masters of the soil, for none were left to share it with them. Portugal, as far as they occupied it, had become part of Napoleon's empire.

About midday a short halt ensued, and while thus resting, a numerous body of the staff of the army galloped by. At the head of this group a remarkable and distinguished-looking officer cast a hawk's-eye glance at our column, as he rapidly passed,—it was Wellington! This first view quite realised my previously conceived idea of the hero of India, of the Douro, and of Talavera, now fresh from the field of Busaco. This then was the mind, which moved not only an army, but a nation in its defence!

On the 5th we continued our retreat and passed through Leyria, the inhabitants of which had already fled; the town was left desolate; confusion and plunder had done their work, and the provost-martial his duty, by hanging two British soldiers detected in the act of robbing. An hour after our column had passed, the French cavalry came up with our rear-guard, and a skirmish ensued. Our Light Artillery were greatly pressed by the enemy, so as at one time to force them to hasten their pace considerably, to avoid being cut off.

After their retreat through the town, large casks of wine were extracted from the cellars and rolled into the streets, so as to block up the road, and by their contents to tempt the new-comers to refresh themselves. This expedient was hit on by Lieutenant-Colonel Elley, D.A. Adjutant-General of Cavalry. Having been sent back with a communication to our rear, I happened to witness the commencement of this scene, which perfectly answered the desired end.

Until now the weather had been fine, although too warm for

us, who were unaccustomed to it; but the evening we arrived at Aldea Gallega, the rains commenced, and came down in torrents such as are seen only in the South. We were forced to follow Corporal Trim's plan, and by an additional allowance (for want of better) of that detestable alcohol, called in Portuguese *agua ardente,* "we kept out the radical moisture by pouring in the radical heat." I slept this night close to my company, on the gentle declivity of a ploughed field; and having taken up my berth in a furrow, found, when I awoke next morning, that it had been turned into a purling stream, which had run in at my stock and out at my boots.

On the 8th we reached the small village of San Quintinho, at the foot of the position which Lord Wellington had long before pointed out and fortified. Here our division, for the first time since I had joined them, was placed under cover. This was the place chosen by Lord Wellington to dispute with the enemy the possession of Portugal, and on this spot hung the future fate of the Peninsula.

On the 9th we halted, and were kept all day in constant readiness to turn out. Next day we moved to Sobral, somewhat in advance of our position, and where the acclivity commences.

On the 11th, accompanied by an engineer officer, I was sent, in command of a working-party of thirty men of my regiment, to mine a small bridge which crossed a stream about five miles from the village of Sobral, toward Torres Vedras. The engineer set us to work, but with most inadequate tools, which were soon rendered useless by the massive stone-work, and the strength of the cement. Whilst thus employed, Sir Lowry Cole's Division (the Fourth) passed in rear of my party; and I perceived a general movement throughout our army, which was occasioned by the advance of the enemy. Our different divisions were moving into the alignment assigned to each: shortly after, a column of French cavalry made their appearance in front of the bridge.

The tools my men had to work with were almost all broken; the engineer officer had left me; the rest of the army were moving to the rear, and a column of the enemy's cavalry was at no great distance in my front: situated as I was, some hours must have elapsed before the work could be accomplished; and no powder had been provided to load the mine when finished. In this dilemma, after due consideration, I determined to retire, as no good could result from our remaining.

We had scarcely come to this determination, when we perceived that some of the enemy's dragoons had passed a ravine to our right, and already occupied the road by which we had come. I now ordered my men to load, and we made for a vineyard, which we gained just as the advance of the column of cavalry had reached the bridge, and joined those who had passed the ravine lower down, and who intended to cut us off.

Sending some of my men to straggle up the slope of the vineyard, as if we had all retired toward the heights, I concealed the others behind a stone wall, within fifty yards of the bridge; and as the enemy reached this, and were crowding upon it to pass, we gave them a well-directed volley, which unseated some, and rolled over the horses of others, and then moved quickly through the vineyard towards the hills. By this time it became quite dark, the rain fell heavily, and a thunderstorm commenced: our uncertain steps were guided, in a pitch dark night, only by the flashes of lightning.

We wandered for hours among these hills, without a track to guide us, or a notion where we were, sliding in the rich clammy soil at every step we took: at last, by mere chance, we stumbled on a small mountain village, the principal house of which had been destined for Lord Wellington's head-quarters. This was Pero Negro.

Here we found out the destination of our brigade from some of Lord Wellington's orderlies belonging to our corps; and having procured a Portuguese guide, in about an hour we rejoined our battalion on the march, whilst wading a mountain-torrent. Shortly after we came to a few miserable cottages, into which our brigade, with one of German artillery, took shelter for the night. We had just made fires to dry and warm ourselves, when we heard an uncommon disturbance in the next hut, which was only divided from that we occupied by a partition of loose stones, doing duty as wall for both dwellings.

It appeared that the ammunition of the German reserve artillery, commanded by Major Hartman[1], had been stowed away in this place, and that the large fire we had lighted had produced considerable alarm, its sparks having found their way through the loose stones into the next apartment, and falling on the caissons of powder: wet blankets were applied, which shortly set all right again. Two Portuguese soldiers, however, who had taken shelter amongst us, as soon as they understood the nature of the danger, made off, and, in spite of the inclemency of the weather, we saw nothing more of them that night.

An hour before daylight on the 12th we stood to our arms, and our baggage was sent to the rear. Daylight broke, but still all was quiet, and our men proceeded to cook their rations. We occupied the ridge of a steep ravine intersected by vineyards; another hill rose in front of this, not quite so high as that on which our line was formed, but sufficiently so to exclude any view of the enemy beneath; we were consequently in like manner hidden from them. On this hill, separated from us by the valley, the advanced posts of our Division were placed, consisting of the 71st Regiment under Colonel Cadogan, and some Portuguese Caçadores; they were supported by the 42nd, the 79th Highlanders, and the 50th Regiment; on the extreme left, in rear of some windmills, lay the Light Infantry of the Guards.

All remained quiet till about midday, when the enemy, after rolling some empty casks up to their advance posts in our front, busied themselves by filling them with earth, and thus made a breast-work, behind which they collected a sufficient force to advance, and make a reconnoissance of our position. They came on with that spirited liveliness with which French troops always move to the attack; but the 71st and the gallant Colonel Cadogan were not slow to meet them, and in conjunction with the Caçadores drove them back.

1. Now General Sir Julius Hartman, commanding the artillery of the King of Hanover.

25

The colonel, at the head of his regiment, leaped his horse over the casks into the midst of the enemy, who were eventually driven down the hill faster even than their ardour brought them up. Thus closed the affair of the day, and no doubt their curiosity was satisfied; as never, whilst we held the position of the lines, did they again show any similar intrusive propensities.

Many English travellers whose curiosity led them at this time to visit our army, being of course non-combatants, were known amongst us by the name of amateurs. The continent of Europe being closed against England, except the footing we had obtained for ourselves in Portugal, most of the young men of travelling propensities used to favour us with their company. It certainly was pleasant to see one's friends and acquaintance, but somewhat troublesome and difficult to dispose of them hospitably and safely, where lodging, feeding, or fighting was in question; we found it awkward, and they no doubt disagreeable.

I remember Lord George Nugent and H. Fox (subsequently attached to our Legation in the United States) reaching the army. Fremantle, the adjutant of the Coldstream, though small in stature, was great in friendship with Lord George, "that young man about town," who arrived at Zibreira when we were all doubled up in a lump in a large *quinta*, the men below, the officers above, six and seven in a room together, He arrived wet, hungry, fatigued and sleepy, and therefore required clothes, food and rest. In size, Nugent was no chicken, and Fremantle, even if he had burst in the attempt, could not, like the frog in the fable, have emulated him in bulk; the difference being somewhat between that of a gallant cock-sparrow and a balloon.

Poor Fremantle was a warm-hearted fellow, replete with suggestive resource, full of fun, and on the occasion of administering to the wants of his friend, proved himself an adaptive (to coin a word) as well as inventive genius. As clothes would not fit, by way of coat he lent his friend his grey cloak, which, from its curt proportions, resembled a mistranslated female garment, of flannel texture, surrounding the colossal shoulders of his full-blown friend. Then, in the most hospitable and friendly manner, he adopted, without leave, that *rara avis in terris*, a cooked turkey (the real property of the battalion surgeon), which had been left, in much negligent simplicity, on the window-seat in the verandah of the *quinta*, in readiness to deck the expectant table of an adjoining mess.

I speak feelingly, as I know those who suffered from the mal-appropriation, "*et j'y étais, j'en sais bien mieux le conte!*" Fremantle and his friends proving more eager ornithologists than the original possessor, the bird was dissected, and the doctor found nothing but its respectable skeleton in a naked dish under his window next morning, considerably left there as an object for his scientific contemplation. Finally Fremantle afforded his friend a corner on the soft side of a deal board, on the floor, in a dormitory, surrounded by the soothing and hush-a-by sounds of five other snoring fellows.

After the affair at Sobral, we moved from Zibreira to our right, and toward our rear to some wretched cabins called *Casaes*. Our village (if a few straggling houses could be dignified by the name), was composed of edifices built by no means with too great a nicety to the exclusion of cold or wet. The one I occupied, which might be taken as a specimen of the whole, was composed of two apartments, an upper and a lower one; the latter was intended for a stable, as is the custom throughout Portugal. Into this the men of the company I belonged to were packed, while in the upper room, divided from the lower region by a floor full of holes and of uncertain solidity, were quartered the captain, myself, another subaltern, and W———, the assistant-surgeon of our battalion, a most enlightened man and charming companion.

An external wooden staircase from the village street led to the half-demolished door of our garret; an opening like that to a hay-loft immediately opposite the entrance served as window, and the tiles, through which many an aperture was visible, admitted wind and water, the rain washing the officers before it reached the men below. Some husks of Indian corn occupied the corner on the left of the door; two others were filled by large wooden chests, formerly enclosing the worldly goods of the poor proprietors, but now made to serve us as table and bed; a knapsack was our pillow, and our cloaks our covering.

A whole army of fleas in close column were in previous possession of this apartment; they took up an imposing position under the corn-husks; we were determined to dislodge them. They disputed the point inch by inch, and the encounter with so formidable a phalanx was not ended without the loss of blood on both sides; and, although the main force had been routed, night after night much desultory skirmishing ensued.

*Oh ye gentlemen of England*
*Who live at home at ease,*
*How little do you think upon*
*The dangers of the—Fleas!*

This, for the best part of five weeks, was our home; the French were more *al fresco,* with certain exceptions, than even we were, and as time jogged on they hutted themselves.

One dark windy night I was on advance piquet, not far from the large central fort; the French sentries after dusk were pushed to within some fifty yards of ours; the orders were, not to fire unless the enemy made a movement in advance; we habitually found them equally civil, and a tacit understanding seemed to exist that we should not shoot one another unless absolutely necessary.

An hour before daylight the general of the brigade visited my piquet; it was a hazy morning, and daylight broke slowly; a fog hung in the dells and over the undulating ground in our front; there was an upright rock at some little distance in advance of the piquet, which looked, in the uncertain light, like a French *vedette* with his long drab cloak; the general fell into this mistake, and thinking the presumed *vedette* had advanced too near, ordered me to fire. Knowing thoroughly the ground in my front, I ventured to assure him of his error, at which insinuation he was pleased to be angry and peremptorily ordered me to obey. Of course my compliance was immediate; but the echo of my

28

sentry's shot came back as flat a denial of the presence of an enemy as the sound of a bullet against a rock could well venture to express in contradiction to a brigadier.

At this moment Lord Wellington rode up; he asked what had occasioned the firing; the brigadier had an awkward excuse to make, and to avow his incorrectness of vision; Lord Wellington, turning sharply round, asked him how old he was; the brigadier replied, "Forty-four."

"Ah!" said Lord Wellington, "you will be a great soldier by the time you are as old as I am."

The future Duke at that time was only forty-one. We remained unmolested in our position, but in constant readiness to meet with prompt attention any visit our opponents might think proper to pay us; for this purpose our men slept in their accoutrements and we in our clothes. An hour before daylight each morning we stood to our arms; the baggage was packed and sent to the rear; clear roads, a clear field, and no *impedimenta*, was the order, and thus we remained till daylight made all objects distinct in the distance.

Lord Wellington was with us almost daily before dawn, and generally took up his post with his telescope near our advance-piquets, or at the large fort which looked down on Sobral and the enemy's posts, till satisfied by personal observation in broad daylight, that no movement of attack was contemplated by the enemy, after which he generally returned to Pero Negro.

In the evening we often rode to the advance-posts, to hear their bands and see their parades; sometimes our gun-boats on the Tagus, under Lieutenant Frederick Berkeley[2], would wake them, up with a cannonade from the river. About this .time Lord Wellington received orders to invest Marshal Beresford with the Grand Cross of the Bath, in honour of which he gave a grand ball and supper at Mafra, to which all officers who could be spared from duty were invited.

Being on out-piquet that day I was not of the party, but I heard it was to be regretted that more hunger than good-breed-

2. Now Admiral Berkeley, M.P. and one of the naval Lords of the Admiralty.

ing was evinced by some of the invited, whose care for themselves was so great as not quite to follow the maxim of "eat what you please, but take nothing away." It would be hard, however, in this instance, that the faults of the few should be visited on the many; at the same time there could be no doubt that, in the too general invitation given by Lord Wellington, stronger marks of the kitchen and pantry preferences than those of the drawing-room were displayed by some of the guests.

On the 14th of November, in the night, after more than a month's sedative contemplation of our heights, our ravines, our forts, our breastworks and mined bridges, Massena broke up from before the lines of Torres Vedras. In vain had he cast a longing look to find a practicable entry,— none such offered, and he retired in disgust: the grapes were sour!

On the 16th we followed, and on our line of march, in the wine-house of a *quinta*, midst empty casks, we found the body of a young French soldier; his face was covered with flies, his figure emaciated, as if he had died from inanition, his uniform in tatters, and without covering he lay on his back upon the ground where he had probably died and was left.

Were it not disgusting by its irreverence, it would have been amusing to see the tricks they played with their own dead, stowing them away in all inconceivable places, enclosing them in large chests, placing them upright in full uniform in the recesses of houses and convents, tying them on to the top of windmills with their arms in their hands, pointed as if levelled at those who advanced, and, worse than all, throwing them down wells; one body, with its shako on, was found seated in the pulpit of a roofless chapel, with its musket in the position of presenting arms.

We reached Alemquer, where some little skirmishing had occurred that morning with the French rear; it was left totally empty, and in an extraordinary condition of filth; no windows, no doors,—all were destroyed for firewood; the weather was inclement as far as rain went, the roads frightful in respect to mud; not an atom of provender for man or beast to be had,

Massena having been starved out of his position before he left it. After seeing our men under cover, several of our officers were huddled, by way of quarter, into the large room of a house in the main street, without fire or the means of making one. In a kind of hiding-place I discovered a sack of Indian corn, and looked on this as a prize for our poor horses and mules, till, on examination, I found fine pieces of glass industriously broken and mischievously mixed amongst it, so that it would have killed an ostrich.

Next day, in equally bad weather, and in the dark, we reached Cartaxo, and were stowed away under cover in an empty convent, with the same facilities of comfort as the previous night.

On the 19th, on assembling we heard that the enemy were only at some eight miles' distance, and that we were to attack them. The morning was fine and the report exciting. Our division, after marching some two hours and a half, came to the turn of a road leading down to a long causeway, which crossed an extensive marsh; above and immediately opposite we once more recognized in line and column and Light-Infantry order, ensconced in olive groves and in a strong position behind abattis, the persons we were seeking to follow with so much trouble in such very bad weather.

The Light Division were to attack on our right, and we were to storm this long causeway. Old Brigadier-General Cameron (afterwards Sir Alan Cameron), who was jealous that our brigade instead of his was destined to lead the division, informed us that, in his opinion, if our brigade were to lead, "there would be very few of His Majesty's Guards left to tell the tale." With this admonition and in a disappointed mood he left us, and we were much amused at the gallant old soldier's manner of expressing his envy at being deprived of the post of honour.

The preparation for attack by the Light Division and ours was all made, and on reaching the head of the causeway of Calhariz, we received orders to load. The causeway was eight hundred yards in length; our orders were to pass the Rio Mayor, over which the bridge and causeway were thrown, in close columns of sections right in front (the width admitting no greater extension), and, on reaching three parts of its length, to jump the parapet on our left down into the marsh, throw out skirmishers, form line quickly, and storm the height before us; the Light Division were to attempt to pass these marshes lower down to our right; and Brigadier-General Craufurd, although he tried to disguise it by hanging on his horse's neck, looked full of impatient anxiety to receive the order to advance,—but it came not.

Owing to a mistake of the road by a brigade of guns[3], the attack could not be made as was intended, and in fact ordered; and in the course of that night and the following morning so much rain had fallen, as to render it impracticable to cross the Rio Mayor and its marshes. We still, however, continued to work on with our troops on the right of the position of Santarem, on which side it appeared most practicable to approach it; until the 22nd, when the enemy brought up troops of the 8th corps from their rear, and drove in our piquets beyond the bridge of Calhariz. From this circumstance, and others, of which we obtained a knowledge about the same time, it was evident that they had their whole army between Santarem and the Zazere, and not merely Regnier's rear-guard, composed of the 2nd Corps.

The question of attacking the enemy on their position of Santarem was then well considered, and the notion was relinquished, as the plan was impracticable at that moment, on account of the state of the roads and rivulets, as well as because it was obvious that the enemy had their whole army collected in certainly the strongest position in Portugal. The original order to attack was only meant to take place on their outposts, to make them show their troops their position, and their intention to hold it. This being countermanded, after three days' occupation of a few houses, called Vallé, on the 23rd of November our Division countermarched to Cartaxo, which was Lord Wellington's head-quarters for the winter. The Light Division was left on outpost duty on our side this famed causeway, in front of Santarem. And thus ended the campaign of 1810.

3. See the Duke of Wellington's *Memorandum of Operations*, No. 504.

# CHAPTER 3

# Campaign of 1811

Head-quarters, Cartaxo, December 1st.

Here we were still riding at single anchor, ready to wait on our neighbours early or late, who, being only at a comfortable country visiting distance, might step in at our breakfast or dinner hour any day; we therefore for some time, both night and day, remained ready dressed and accoutred to meet them, and pay all possible and necessary attention to their requirements, and that at the shortest possible notice.

In time things became more settled, and, finding that our French neighbours had become domesticated in their abode, and had ostensibly settled themselves down during the rainy season and bad weather, we in turn began to think of rendering ourselves a little more comfortable than empty houses, shutterless windows, and hinges without doors were likely to allow. We set about in our quarters improving the property of the inhabitants during their absence; for as yet they had not returned.

As no fireplaces existed, we built chimneys (assisted by the ingenious bricklayers of our corps), repaired doors, made window-frames and filled them with oiled paper. We concocted portable tables and chairs, and stretchers for bedsteads; and at last, after sleeping for three months in our clothes, actually had sufficient confidence and hardihood to go to bed. I shall never forget the comfortless feeling experienced in confiding my person, for the first time, to a pair of cold stark naked sheets. I could not sleep a wink. But at length we accustomed ourselves to repose in our beds, although all were prepared, at a moment's notice, to turn out of them.

Our men were quartered in an empty monastery on entering the town by the road from Lisbon, our officers in the houses near them. Sir Brent Spencer, who commanded our division, had a strange aversion to the noise of drums, and, in winter-quarters, ordered them on no account to beat. By some accident a bell, unstolen and unbroken, had been left by the French in the belfry of the empty monastic dwelling appropriated as a quarter for one of the battalions; their adjutant, Fremantle[1], who particularly disliked Sir Brent's partiality for silence, was somewhat puzzled how the men and officers were to be warned for assembly; and, as he could not drum them, he satisfied himself by ordering the drummer to toll his battalion to parade.

When it came to his knowledge, this ingenious substitute amused Lord Wellington much; it certainly was ridiculous enough on week-days (although more appropriate on Sundays) to assemble thus. Lord Wellington was very regular in attending divine service at our church parade, but always limited the time of its duration, saying to the chaplain, "Briscal, say as much as you like in five-and-twenty minutes, I shall not stay longer."

This winter I frequently dined with Lord Wellington, and, on the first occasion of doing so, my attention was naturally fixed on observing the manners and conversation of our chief; they seemed perfectly natural, straightforward and open. He conversed with liveliness on most subjects. There was at this period a light-heartedness of manner about him, which betokened more of self-confidence than anxiety or care, and which gave an agreeable tone to the society around him.

Although upon his acts depended the fate of nations, few, from observation, could discover that he felt himself in a more responsible position than the youngest subaltern of his army. He seemed to enjoy the boyish tricks of those about him; weighty affairs did not appear to have impaired his zest for the playfulness or jokes of his followers. At table he seldom spoke of mili-

---

1. Fremantle, previously and afterwards A.D.C. to the Duke of Wellington.

tary matters, and never of passing events in Portugal; the news of the day from England, the amusements, or social state of Lisbon, or allusions to foreign countries, most frequently formed the topics of his conversation.

One day I met there Mr. Sydenham, a friend of Lord Wellington's, lately arrived on a visit to him. In the course of conversation at table, this gentleman expressed his satisfaction at Lord Wellington's apparent good looks and health, and added: "With the details you have to think of, the numerous affairs, both political and diplomatic, you have to provide for, added to the military responsibility you have to bear, I cannot conceive how you can sleep in your bed?"—

"When I throw off my clothes I throw off my cares, and when I turn in my bed it is time to turn out," was Lord Wellington's short and characteristic reply.

The sudden change from a state of action and excitement, where daily difficulties were to be overcome or daily wants provided for, to one of comparative inactivity in our winter-quarters, was flat and unprofitable. Without books or anything to break the *tedium vita,* the arrival of a mail from England was the great event. When newspapers reached us they were read with avidity; they contained old news of ourselves, besides endless speculative opinions on the result of the war, each in the plenitude of their simplicity, or, according to their own political views and interests. With one we were all glorious and successful, with another Lord Wellington was an ignoramus and we were all going to a place not to be named in print.

On this account I know no position more irksome than that of an English general commanding an army in a distant foreign land. He has his country's enemies before him and his country's friends behind-him, and it is difficult to say which show him, or desire to show him, less mercy. I am inclined to think the easier of the two to deal with is the enemy in front. Pew can tell the harm that was done during this war by newspaper reports and extracts from the letters of officers from Lisbon and elsewhere, lingerers about the hospitals and depots, men ignorant and discontented, who wrote all kind of trash, which by force of transit across the waves was transformed into "important intelligence." Lord Wellington, in writing on this subject to his brother the Minister in Spain, Mr. Henry Wellesley, from Pero Negro, says,

> The freedom of the Press is undoubtedly a benefit, and it is difficult possibly to fix the limits beyond which it shall not go. But if the benefit consists in the information which the Press conveys to the nation and the world in general, it appears to be necessary that the information should be founded in fact, and that discussions upon the conduct of military operations and the characters of officers who carry them on, should be founded on real knowledge of events, of the true state of affairs, of the character of the troops, and above all of the topography of the country which may be the seat of the operations.

Every Englishman admires and would support the freedom of the Press; but as discretion is the better part of valour, so ought it to be of the power of journalism, as there is no end to the mischief that may be done for five-pence. The enemy frequently gained intelligence of importance to them through our papers, of which otherwise they would have been wholly ignorant; and at one time Lord Wellington even, in a despatch to Lord Liverpool, expressed a hope that his own despatches would not, on this account, be fully published.

Personal considerations now began to have weight with us, and our happiest hours were when the evening closed in and we met together; the inhabitants had begun to return to their homes, provisions had become more plentiful, and when dinner (the best we could provide) was served in our separate quarters among the various coteries, many a young happy face shone by the light of our merry wood fire-many a joyous evening of mirth and laughter was passed by the side of our stone chimney.

Those days, alas! are now long gone: the space of nearly half a century is creeping on between them and us: different fates betided the different beings who then were warmed by the cheery spirit of youth and Lamego wine. Hopes, like our blood, ran high and gilded the future for us; but time and reality have cast deep shadows over those early aspirations.

Where now amongst immediate friends are to be found Crofton, Jack Fremantle, George Fitz-Clarence, Paulet Mildmay, Gurwood, Tom Bligh, Wentworth Burges? All gone! The first fell in the sortie of Bayonne, the last in an enemy's embrasure, leading a storming-party at Burgos; the third of these died a member of the Upper House, the fourth a member of the House of Commons; Fremantle a general, Gurwood a secretary to the Duke of Wellington; and poor Tom Bligh died, not as he wished, in the field, but of protracted consumption at Valence. Alas! time has made sad havoc among friends as well as foes; but memory peoples the earth again with them, calling back to mind all their wit, humour, hilarity, and good feeling, till one is tempted, as in the *ci-devant jeune homme,* to exclaim, *"Oh! ma jeunesse, ma jeunesse, où est ma jeunesse?"*

On the 23rd of January the Marquis de la Romana died suddenly, from bursting a blood-vessel, as he was dressing to dine with Lord Wellington. He had arrived not long before at Cartaxo in bad health, having left his corps of 10,000 men in the Alemtejo and at Badajoz. He was greatly regretted, being one of the best, if not the best, of the Spanish generals. Lord Wellington wrote:

> In him the Spanish army have lost their brightest ornament, his country their most upright patriot, and the world the most strenuous and zealous defender of the cause in which we are engaged; and I shall always acknowledge with gratitude the assistance which I received from him, as well by his operations as by his counsel, since he had been joined with this army.

Lord Wellington and his staff, besides many other officers, attended the removal of the body, which was taken down, on the carriage of a six-pounder gun, in funeral procession to Velhada on the Tagus. On this occasion I made the acquaintance of a very amiable man and gallant soldier, who not only acted but evidently felt as a chief mourner for his departed friend. General *Don* Miguel Alava had to deplore not alone the loss he had personally sustained, but that by which his country might suffer.

The surrendering of Badajoz a few months after through treachery amply realised his fears. This Spanish nobleman's fate was singularly chequered. He had fought against Nelson at the battle of Trafalgar, under Gravina; on our entering Portugal and Spain he was attached to Lord Wellington, as Spanish *aide-de-camp*, to communicate with the Spanish armies, and during the whole of the Peninsular War he remained in the same post. His estates near Vittoria had been plundered and taken possession of by the French, and the battle subsequently fought there was on part of his property. When the war was over he returned to Madrid; and Ferdinand the Seventh, merely because he gave his Majesty some honest advice concerning the Cortes, rewarded his services by putting him in prison, where he remained forty days in close confinement.

At the personal and urgent interference of the Duke of Wellington he was liberated; he afterwards became ambassador from the grateful monarch who had incarcerated him, to Louis the Eighteenth, and on the return of Napoleon to France he attended his Majesty in his flight from Paris to Ghent. Alava was present, in attendance on his old chief the Duke, at the battle of Waterloo, although he was diplomatically attached to the King of France. Here he was again wounded, notwithstanding which he dictated a despatch to his sovereign, one of the best and most eloquently descriptive of any published of that great event.

Soon after Waterloo I met him at Paris, at the table of the late King of Holland (then Prince of Orange); they had been brother *aides-de-camp* to the Duke in the Peninsula, and their intimacy was great; the party was small, the weather was hot, and the wine was cool. Old times were talked of; position was forgotten, and sociability prevailed; the conversation was on the late great action, when the Prince said, forgetting that his old friend was now the representative of the Spanish monarch. "Ah!

Alava, what would the Spaniards have done, had they been at Waterloo?"

"Very much what the Belgians did, your Royal Highness."

In 1823, Alava formed one of the Cortes, and was at Cadiz with King Ferdinand; being a clever and moderate man, he did his best to accommodate matters on the arrival of the French under the Duke d'Angoulême, but he found it impossible, from the uncommon want of honesty in the character of King Ferdinand. Again he was exiled, his estates were confiscated, and he remained in banishment until recalled by the Queen Regent, on his being named to the Cortes. During his exile he principally resided in England, and was a constant guest of his old friend the Duke of Wellington, both at Apsley House and at Strathfieldsaye.

But to return from this digression, we frequently rode to our outposts at the causeway, where our sentries and those of the enemy were placed, quite within conversational distance of each other. The French officers at first came across and conversed with ours, and even invited them into Santarem, to attend theatricals they had got up among themselves. An order from Lord Wellington however put a stop to this; for, although evil communication may not always corrupt good manners, it is just possible that the very purest intercourse may be the means of conveying inconvenient intelligence.

Among the idle Clubs, which an assembly of officers off duty was called, there was a story current at the outposts concerning the assistant adjutant-general of the Light Division, who, at the table of General Craufurd, his chief, used to ask the invited guests to drink wine, and looking the object of his intended attention full in the face would say, "Captain Taylor, a glass of wine?" The officers, on comparing notes, found that in like manner all had been so baptised, the fact being that Captain ——— called every officer whose name he did not know, whatever his rank might be, "Captain Taylor."

When spoken to on this subject by a friend, he replied, "Well now, what would you have me do? I don't know that their names are not Taylor; there is great probability that I guess right, and sometimes there is applicability when probability is wanting; and as for captain, as Gibbet says in the play, 'that is a good travelling name' and so when I don't know a man, I always call him Captain Taylor. Were I to call out Smith or Brown, it might create confusion. Taylor is more exclusive, and fits better; there are many of that breed most distinguished, from Stultz downwards."

Such was the prattle of a merry, gallant, amusing, good-looking, and active man,—now a portly, good-natured *bon vivant* general, who has served in three out of the four quarters of the globe.

This winter Cornet Strenuwitz, of the Hanoverian Hussars, particularly distinguished himself on outpost duty, taking prisoners a whole French piquet, considerably more numerous than his own, without losing a single one of his party: he discovered that they were too far removed from their supports, and in the night he cut them off. To be outdone in alertness and manoeuvre annoyed *Messieurs les Français* much; retaliation is sweet, and they laid a plan to circumvent the cornet. Unluckily for them, Strenuwitz knew the country even better than they did; and, having gained intelligence of their intention from a deserter, when in a dark night they advanced round his flank to carry off their prize, he and his piquet were nowhere to be found.

Disliking to advance too far, for fear of coming on our supports, the enemy were prudently drawing back towards their own outposts, when they were surprised by a dashing charge, and cut down by a body of cavalry, coming from the very point on which they were directing their retreat: all of them, including their officer, were brought in prisoners to Cartaxo, more or less wounded. Lord Wellington was much pleased at this conduct, named Strenuwitz in his despatches, and recommended him for promotion[2].

In spite of their occasional *rencontres*, when brought into accidental proximity, the French and English soldiers showed them-

---

2. He afterwards distinguished himself in a cavalry encounter in the south of Spain.

selves noble enemies, and betrayed far greater estimation of the national qualities each possessed, than they did of the countries the latter were sent to defend and the former to conquer. This feeling was observable during many opportunities of intercourse on outpost duty,—symptoms of it were displayed in small acts of courtesy.

An officer of the 16th Light Dragoons (whose name not having noted at the time I forget,) had, on making a reconnoissance, remained imprudently somewhat too long in observation of one of the enemy's advance guards. On his attention being drawn to his flank, he perceived that, if he did not gallop for it, he would be cut off from his own piquet and made prisoner. It had rained all night—he was enveloped in a well-saturated cloak, which embarrassed his movements, and added to the weight his horse had to carry. Before setting spurs to his charger, therefore, he at once unclasped his mantle and let it fall to the ground; and thus lightening himself and steed he escaped.

Some few days afterwards, a French dragoon was seen to advance towards our outposts; he approached one of our *vedettes* as near as he thought prudent, and making a sign to him, let fall something, and rode back under cover of his own advance-posts. On examination it was found to be the cloak, abandoned by the officer of the 16th a few days previously, his name and regiment being marked on it. Many other similar acts of good feeling and politeness came to my knowledge during my services.

Amongst others of my comrades I was a sportsman; woodcocks were numerous, and snipes were to be found on the low marshy grounds. We had at this time no dogs, but Lord Wellington kindly allowed officers of his acquaintance to take his; and we frequently did so, to our pleasure and profit; as not only the sport, but the result of it, when a good bag was made, was most acceptable, where luxuries for the table by no means abounded: many a pleasant hour was thus passed, which tended to maintain our good health, and increase our good cheer.

In preparation for a day's sport, two of us were seated one fine morning at breakfast in my quarter, which was on the right hand, half-way down the main street, on entering the town from Lisbon; the windows looked on the street, but at the back there was an open space or kind of yard, with a well in common to many houses adjoining: we were in a hurry to proceed to our day's sport, but found our servants dilatory in making the necessary preparations for us.

After sundry hailings and ejaculations, symptomatic of our impatience, one of our people at last came to us, with a face in which was depicted surprise, risibility, and disgust. On our inquiring what had happened, he replied, "Oh, we have got him out!"

"Got whom out?" we asked.

"Why, sir, in drawing water, I had the misfortune to drop the camp-kettle into the well, and in trying to fish it out with a hook, I pulled up by the collar of his great-coat a dead French infantry soldier!"

We had been drinking the water for a month! About this time we received a supply of Congreve rockets from England, which were to be experimented on by our army. Lord Wellington, thinking the enemy the best butt to try them against, rode down to a low, marshy piece of ground, which ran between the river and the heights of Santarem, and was separated from the town and French position by the confluence of the Rio Mayor with the Tagus.

We commenced operations, at which, amongst others, I happened to be present. The wind was high, and blowing freshly in our teeth; the height to which the rockets were to be directed necessitated a proportionate degree of elevation: live shells were attached to each rocket. After considerable preparation they were discharged; but, to our no small inconvenience, instead of prosecuting their flight toward the enemy, the wind carried them perpendicularly up, and then brought two of them back amongst us: this made a scurry, and we galloped off in different directions, to give room for the shells to explode harmlessly.

After this trial Lord Wellington, in the Peninsular campaigns, made no further use of deadly weapons of such uncertain direction; even in Belgium, in 1815, a brigade of rockets was sent out to him; but he turned three parts of the brigade into guns, saying, that he "preferred nine-pounders."

On riding one day toward our outposts, to our left, in the direction of Azambuja, we saw, on reaching them, a number of French staff-officers collected in our front. Amongst these was a marshal of France, whom we recognized by his *chapeau plumé:* they approached our advanced sentries, and at first rode along them; when the marshal, through his telescope, began to reconnoitre our ground, and the troops which held it. After this he once more approached, and came within some two hundred yards of our out-sentry, belonging to the Portuguese *Caçadores*.

This was considered a little too familiar, and displayed an intention of becoming more intimately acquainted with us and our situation than we felt inclined to permit of. The officer on duty, an English captain in the Portuguese service, waved his hand to the *cortège* of French staff-officers, as a polite signal for them to retire; but the Marshal and his Staff paid no attention to the obliging hint: this neglect induced our captain to order his sentry to fire, which he did so successfully as to bring the marshal immediately down from his horse, the shot having passed through his face. It was Junot who was thus wounded; and the English captain of Caçadores gave the sentry who made the shot a dollar, as a mark of his consideration for the correct view he had taken of things in his front.

On the 4th of March, 1811, a private of the 24th Regiment was condemned by a court-martial to be hanged for desertion and theft. The sentence was carried into execution on the 5th, in presence of detachments of the regiments of the First Division, to which the culprit belonged, and the following order was promulgated from head-quarters.

Adjutant-General's Office, Cartaxo,<br>March 4th, 1811.

1. As the object in assembling troops in any station to witness a punishment, is to deter others from the commission of the crime for which the criminal is about to suffer, the

Commander of the Forces requests that, upon every occasion on which troops are assembled for this purpose, the order may be distinctly read and explained to them, and that every man may understand the reason for which the punishment is inflicted.

2. As, for the two years during which the Brigade of Guards have been under the command of the Commander of the Forces, not only no soldier has been brought to trial before a general court-martial, but no one has been confined in a public guard, the Commander of the Forces desires that the attendance of this brigade at the execution tomorrow may be dispensed with.

Rumours came of the enemy being about to move; and having lost a valuable baggage-mule on our advance from the lines to the causeway of Calhariz, I now made it good by purchasing two at head-quarters, from Lord March[3].

On the night of the 5th of March, the campaign of 1811 commenced, by the enemy breaking up from their position at Santarem, and beginning their retreat from Portugal. Every military motive existed to induce them to have taken this step long before, and they should have continued their retreat when they broke up from before the lines; but political reasons outweighed all other considerations.

Applying a commonplace phrase to the explanation of a diplomatic motive,—"What would Mrs. Grundy have said" had they at once abandoned their original intentions, and retired from Portugal without a semblance of retaining it? Now all Europe, and Spain in particular, was Napoleon's Mrs. Grundy, in whose eyes he did not wish to display either weakness or failure. If the enemy preferred remaining cut off from their supplies and communications, and starving a little longer, instead of falling back to refit and refresh themselves for a future struggle, we of course could have no objection, especially as we were near our own supplies.

---

3. The present Duke of Richmond.

The patience, prudence, and self-denial of our chief, in for-bearing to attack the enemy, and in bearing the opprobrium cast on him in consequence by the ignorant or foolish in England, were remarkable, but were now amply rewarded; for, ill support-ed and inadequately supplied as he had been by the ministers of that day, still, by husbanding his resources, he had gained his object without risk or bloodshed, and all was prepared to follow up the enemy

On the 6th, after three months' halt, and at half an hour's warning, we left Cartaxo. Every corps of our army was now in full pursuit of the enemy. We entered Santarem, which had been the head-quarters of the French army during the winter. We found things in better order than we expected, with the excep-tion of a few houses the enemy had gutted and burned: among other transmutations we found a church turned into a theatre, with appropriate decorations!

It was a fine, well-built town, superior in size and situation to Cartaxo. As this last place will probably not again be mentioned, I may here say that the British troops sent to Portugal by Can-ning, in 1827, found the town so little changed or improved, that even the names of the officers, and the official quarters as-signed to them, were still to be found written in chalk on doors and window-shutters, as they had been left in the year 1810! For seventeen years they had remained uneffaced from the different houses: was this laziness, economy of soap and water, or for love of "auld lang syne"? I doubt the latter.

We reached Purnes on the 7th, and halted the 8th. It was a pretty village, romantically situated, with a stream running through it, and with some picturesque waterfalls not far distant. This village was in a wretched condition; the few inhabitants left in it, who either could not or would not fly on the advance of the French, or who had attempted a return to their homes during the occupation of the enemy, were absolutely starving; they had been robbed of all they had, and every violence had been done them.

If the result of the advance of the French into Portugal was calamitous, the scenes witnessed on their retreat were deplorable. Destruction, incendiarism, violation, and murder,—in short, desolation, marked their course. Their steps were traced by the conflagration of towns, villages, and *quintas*. From the mountain-heights might be seen to rise the smoke from the valleys, where the habitation of the peasant and mansion of the noble were alike consumed. If the enemy could not exist in the country, they had determined that nothing should be left for others.

Well might Lord Wellington, at this time, write as follows to Lord Liverpool, in reply to financial objections for supplying the necessary men and materials to prosecute the war in the Peninsula. He says, under date of Santa Marinha, 23rd of March, 1811:—

I shall be sorry if Government should think themselves under the necessity of withdrawing from this country, on account of the expense of the contest. From what I have seen of the objects of the French Government, and the sacrifices they make to accomplish them, I have no doubt that, if the British army were for any reason to withdraw from the Peninsula, and the French Government were relieved from the pressure of military operations on the Continent, they would incur all risks to land an army in his Majesty's dominions.

Then, indeed, would commence an expensive contest; then would his Majesty's subjects discover what are the miseries of war, which, by the blessing of God, they have hitherto, had no knowledge of; and the cultivation, the beauty, and prosperity of the country, and the virtues and happiness of its inhabitants, would be destroyed, whatever might be the result of the military operations.

God forbid that I should be a witness, much less an actor in the scene! and I only hope that the King's Government will consider well what I have above stated to your lordship; will ascertain, as nearly as is in their power, the actual expense of employing a certain number of men in this country, beyond that of employing them at home, or elsewhere; and will keep up their force here on such a footing as will, at all events, secure their possession, without keeping the transports, if it does not enable their commander to take advantage of events, and assume the offensive.

The French being unable longer to occupy Portugal, Massena declared he would render it not worth living in; and, as far as lay in his power, he kept his word. On the 9th our division moved by Torres Novas, through a bleak and dreary country, in bad weather, and did not reach Pialva, where we halted for the night, till ten o'clock p.m.

On the 10th, again, through bad weather and worse roads, we followed in the enemy's track to Caçares. On the 11th, after being on the march from half-past six in the morning until ten o'clock at night, we bivouacked in the vicinity of Pombal. Being sent to communicate an order to one of our other brigades, I met in the dark, in an olive grove, a heavy dragoon of ours who had lost his way. He asked me where he "could find head-quarters:" the cavalry-man, to my surprise, had an English officer, in the uniform of his regiment, tied to his back.

This was Lieutenant ———, an Irish Catholic, belonging to the —th regiment, who had not long before deserted to the enemy, and had been retaken in the skirmish at Pombal that morning, and was now being conveyed a prisoner, to Lord Wellington. It was proved, afterwards, that the man was insane; and we had the satisfaction never to hear anything more of him.

From the 11th to the 15th there were very sharp affairs daily between the enemy and the Light, Third, Fourth, and Fifth Divisions, at Pombal, Redinha, Condexa, Miranda, Foz d'Aronce, and the Ceira River. The commencement of that at Redinha was fine in the extreme. The day was clear and bright, the mountainous tract of country beautiful, and the ground on which we deployed and moved forward under fire of the enemy's guns, was extensive in space and grand in view.

The Light Division were hard at work, as they always were, skirmishing with activity; the curling smoke rising from the hollow; the sharp rattle of musketry ascending from the woods and the valleys beneath our front; the booming of cannon-shot through the air, and the echo of the whole from the distant hills; the solemn advance of our supports in three lines; by division, backed by columns,—oh! it was a noble and gallant sight to look upon, more like some pleasant movement of troops in review, than the deadly and destructive reality of strife; but, as we gained ground, the results, though favourable, left behind their marks of mischief.

We marched past the dead, the dying, or the wounded, to that success which, at the time, made those casualties less heeded by the unharmed; but, like some rattling leap taken in a fox-chase, it did not do in sober mind to look back on what you had gone over. The day was gained, the fatigue was passed, and rest at a merry bivouac fire refreshed the weary for the coming day and contest. They both came, but that of the morrow was not so exciting.

The enemy, believing a larger force was on the north bank of the Mondego than merely Wilson and Grant's outposts, and having made some ineffectual attempts to pass the bridge at Coimbra, and some fords where they met resistance, abandoned their idea of retreating in that direction: and as the Third Division now hung on their left flank, they took the road from Condexa to the Puente de Murcella, burning Condexa as they passed through it.

CHAPTER 4

# Entry Into Spain

The following day was the affair of Casal Nova. Early dawn brought with it an intense fog, which lasted for some time after sunrise; our chief having no taste for blindman's buff, we remained on our ground, unable to move; gradually the mountain-tops began to show their heads, looking like so many islets swimming in the sea of fog beneath.

At length the dense mass of mist rose, like a great curtain, from the valleys below, when was displayed to our longing eyes the glorious sight of the whole French rear-guard in martial array, in position, with the sun brightly glittering on their arms. It was a sight enough to make a dolt a soldier! We moved—the same scene of sharp contest ensued— the Light Division ever gallantly sticking to them, and carrying all before them; driving the enemy from hill to hill, across ravines, over streams, from valley to mountain, as we kept moving on in support, occasionally halting, and then again moving rapidly forward.

The Light and Fourth Divisions had turned the enemy's left; our division, and the Fifth and Sixth, the heavy cavalry and artillery, moved on their centre. The French retreat at last became more rapid than regular; confusion ensued amongst them; but they gained the Pass of Miranda, burnt the town, and passed the Ceira that night. Their army was now compressed and crowded into one narrow line, between the high sierras and the Mondego river: they destroyed part of their baggage and ammunition, and left Marshal Ney to cover the passage with a few battalions.

We passed over the ground gained by our gallant light troops: the wounded who could not move to the rear were with the dead, lying as they fell. Among the former were to be found three brothers—those noble fellows, the Napiers, William and George, of the 43rd and 52nd, were lying, severely wounded, not for from the roadside; and Charles, who commanded the 50th, came up at this moment and joined his brothers, not being himself quite recovered from the wound he had received at Busaco. Here, then, were three of one family met together, each bearing on his person the most emphatic mark of having done his duty to his country!

They are now all general officers and Knights of the Bath, and have well earned their distinctions[1]. Sir Charles, previous to this, had been left for dead on the field of Coruna, and was so returned in the list of casualties: he had been found, however, by a Spanish peasant, and taken to his house, recovered, and, by the kindness of Marshal Soult, was liberated.

On his return home, he found his family had been in mourning for him. His after career and services, in annexing Scinde, by conquest, to our Indian empire; and his brother William's merits as a soldier, and as the historian of the Peninsular war, are too well known and appreciated to need any remark from the writer of these pages; he may be allowed however to express his admiration of the talents of this distinguished family, who from, and long before, the days of the great inventor of logarithms, Napier of Merchistoun, whether by sea, by land, or in diplomacy, serve their country to advantage, and never lose sight of their family motto;

*Ready, aye ready.*

Near the Napiers, among others lying wounded, was Captain Jones, a Welshman, and an acquaintance of mine: surgeons were scarce, which is generally the case when troops are skirmishing over a wild, broken, and extensive country, in extended order. Jones was badly hurt, and, at my suggestion, our colonel allowed

---

1. Sir Charles since this as written is dead..

our assistant-surgeon to look at him, on condition of the doctor's immediate return, as we were hurrying on, and knew not how soon we might want his assistance. I believe this medical officer aided the Napiers in their necessity, as well as Captain Jones; and if so, to this hour they know not who sent him.

The following day, the enemy having retired in the night, we did not come up with them till four o'clock p.m. They had been cooking when our advanced guard reached them. Lord Wellington arrived; and, casting a rapid glance at their strong position, ordered an instant attack.

The Light and Third Divisions advanced immediately, and rather disturbed their culinary occupations, which were found in matured preparation, kettles and all on the fires. The visit of our advanced troops being too sudden to give them time to carry off their provisions, our people appropriated these to themselves, and followed the foe,—the Light Division and Packe's Portuguese attacking their right flank, on rough and rugged ground, the Third Division their left, which rested on the village of Foz d'Aronce. The Horse Artillery, galloping forward to a rising ground, opened their fire with a sudden and great effect. Ney's left wing was surprised, and fled in great confusion, rushing down to the bridge and ford, and were crushed to death or drowned in considerable numbers'[2].

We had a rapid scamper of two miles at double-quick after the enemy this evening across the country, through muddy lanes, encumbered with asses and mules, which, incapable of further moving, had been hamstrung, and were thus maimed, poor brutes, to render them useless to us. Through thick pine-woods, without being able to see anything, we followed *au pas accéléré*, direct toward our front, where the usual music prevailed; but in spite of all our efforts, we arrived only in time for Nightingale's brigade of our division to take a share in the fray, which was a sufficiently heavy one.

Darkness now prevailed, and was increased by the gloom of the pine-forest; the firing still continued, and we could see the

2. See *Napier.*

flickering of musketry between the trees, throwing uncertain and indistinct light on the objects around. The Light Division had driven the French rearguard across the Ceira River with great loss. In the dark, one French brigade fired into another; they blew up their spare ammunition, buried some guns, destroyed their baggage, lost an eagle, and suffered severely in killed and wounded in this action. Massena retired behind the Alva, yet Ney maintained the left bank of the Ceira until their remaining encumbrances passed. Thus terminated the first part of the retreat from Santarem.

After this we took some five hundred more prisoners, who had been on a marauding excursion. Our division had been in support of Picton's. Our bivouac was in the pine-wood; we were ordered to make no fires, we had no provisions, our baggage was not allowed to come up. It rained hard throughout the night, but we were directed to make ourselves as comfortable as we could. Next day some of us got a portion of donkey-flesh, cut from the corpses of those respectable animals left behind by the enemy, but minus salt, biscuit, or other addenda; however, it was something, which was better than nothing.

For the rest, we had been successful; for the result of these operations was, that Coimbra and Upper Beira were saved from the enemy's ravages, and they were obliged to take for their retreat the road by the Ponte de Murcella, which enabled the Portuguese Militia, under Wilson and Trant, to manoeuvre on the right bank of the Mondego, which they had already prevented the enemy from passing, and they further continued to act severely on their flank, while the Allied Army still pressed on their rear. They had no provisions except what they plundered on the spot, and carried on their backs; they still continued burning and destroying all they passed through of towns, villages, *quintas*, and houses.

While halting for further supplies from our commissariat, near the banks of the Alva, I found in a roofless house, which had been destroyed by the flames, a poor old man, lying on his own threshold, shot through the body; a young woman, apparently *enceinte,* suspended by the neck to a beam; and a child of tender age, lying at her feet, with its throat cut. And this was "glorious war" as carried on by the French army in Portugal, *anno Domini* 1811!

Lord Wellington, about this date, writes on this subject as follows to Lord Liverpool:—

> I am concerned to be obliged to add to this account, that their conduct throughout this retreat has been marked by a barbarity seldom equalled, and never surpassed. Even in the towns of Torres Novas, Thomar, and Purnes, in which the head-quarters of some of the corps had been for four months, and in which the inhabitants had been invited, by promises of good treatment, to remain, they were plundered, and many of their houses destroyed, on the night the enemy withdrew from their position; and they have since burnt every town and village through which they have passed.
>
> The convent of Alcobaça was burnt by order from the French head-quarters; the bishop's palace, and the whole town of Leyria, in which General Drouet had had his head-quarters, shared the same fate; and there is not an inhabitant of the country, of any class or description, who has had any dealing or communication with the French army, who has not had reason to repent of it and to complain of them. This is the mode in which the promises have been performed, and the assurances have been fulfilled, which were held out in the proclamation of the French commander-in-chief; in which he told the inhabitants of Portugal that he was not come to make war upon them, but with a powerful army of 110,000 men to drive the English into the sea.
>
> It is to be hoped that the example of what has occurred in this country will teach the people of this and of other nations what value they ought to place on such promises and assurances; and that there is no security for life, or for anything which makes life valuable, excepting in decided

resistance to the enemy.

*"Gallis fidem non habendam; hominibus levibus, perfidis, et in ip-sos Deos immortales impiis"* said Cicero some two thousand years ago; and so might the Portuguese people have well said of the descendants of these very Gauls.

We crossed the Sierra de Moita, and moved down to the banks of the Alva; here, having no further commissariat resources, we were obliged to halt, to await their arrival. To save land-transport, and to have our munitions nearer, they were sent round from the Tagus in transports to Mondego Bay.

We had out-marched our provisions, in addition to which the Portuguese Government had, as usual, failed in supplying their own troops, who were then obliged to be furnished by our commissariat; added to this, some of the new and tardily-expedited reinforcements from England (which regiments ought to have reached us before we left Cartaxo), on their way up, against every order to the contrary, seized the commissariat supplies intended for us, and at this critical moment we were left without the means of following the enemy. Our division had in consequence to halt, from the 19th, when we reached Sarzadas, to the 25th of March. On this occasion Lord Wellington wrote as follows:—

> In the night the enemy destroyed the bridge on the Ceira and retreated, leaving a small rear-guard on the river. The destruction of the bridge at Foz d'Aronce, the fatigues which the troops have undergone for several days, and the want of supplies have induced me to halt the army this day?

Again he writes, under date of Gouvea, March 27th:

> When I found that the enemy retired with such celerity from Moita, I continued the pursuit of them with the cavalry and Light Division, supported by the Third and Sixth Divisions; and I was induced to halt the rest of the army till the supplies came up.

We all shared alike in commons so short, and were glad, when we could get it, to have an addition of bullock's liver by way of a luxury. Neither Indian corn, bread, nor biscuit, was to be seen; and I remember giving a dollar for a ship's biscuit to a sergeant of the 42nd, who was coming up from the rear. During this recess from fighting, we heard from Lord March (who complained that nothing was going on) of the battle of Barossa, and, as a counterpoise to this, of the loss of Badajoz, surrendered by the Spaniards on the very day after the governor had received Lord Wellington's assurance that he should be relieved.

It was thought that the commandant had his price; for, except a small breach, the defences were entire, and the guns still mounted. Had Romana lived to be there, this surrender, in all human probability, would not have occurred. We now hutted ourselves during our halt; and being refreshed, provisioned, and washed in the river Alva, where our battalion was daily marched down for the purpose of ablution, we once more moved in advance from Sarzadas and Moita on Celerico.

On the 29th, the Third, Sixth, and Light Divisions again advanced, to attack the enemy in the strong mountain position of Guarda. The wings of these divisions were supported, on the one side, by the Portuguese Militia, on the other, by the Fifth Division; while ours and the newly-formed Seventh moved on the enemy's centre. The French, being thus turned on either flank, retreated in confusion from this formidable post without firing a shot.

On the 1st of April we moved toward the Coa: Wilson and Trant passed it below Almeida to our left; the cavalry crossed the upper Coa on the right; the Light Division were ordered to ford a little below; and the Fifth, with the artillery, to force the bridge of Sabugal. Our Division and the Seventh were in reserve, except a battalion sent to the bridge of Seceiras. It was conjectured that, after the enemy had quitted the position of Guarda without firing a shot, and had passed the Coa, they would continue their retreat without attempting to resist the passage of the river, especially as both Wilson and Trant, and our cavalry, had already passed it on both their flanks.

On the 3rd, in anticipation of our division occupying Sabugal, I was sent forward with our brigade-major to take up quarters for my regiment. We met Colonel Jackson[3], quarter-master-general of our division, who informed us we might save ourselves the trouble of proceeding further, as the French were still in possession of the town; and that, in consequence of the fog, Colonel Waters had just been taken by the enemy's light cavalry.

This being reported to Lord Wellington, he said, "Ah! they have caught him, but they will not keep him."

The prognostication showed how well he knew those under him. Waters, on being made prisoner, which occurred in the haze of the morning, from mistaking in the mist a French patrol for Portuguese troops, was conducted before Marshal Massena; who examined him very closely concerning our movements and intentions—but gained very little information for his pains. The marshal then offered him his parole, which Waters refused to accept: he was allowed however to retain his horse, a famous mare he called the Bittern;[4] and, under a cavalry escort, was marched a close prisoner to Ciudad Rodrigo.

On reaching tins town he happened to be quartered, or rather confined, in the room of a house, the proprietor of which he had formerly known; he seized an opportunity, and requested the Spaniard to get the rowels of his spurs sharpened, which was accomplished without the suspicion of those who guarded him.

Soon after this, he was conducted from Ciudad Rodrigo on his way to Salamanca between two *gendarmes;* while thus situated, at the head of one column of infantry, and in the rear of another, one of the *gendarmes* halted and dismounted to tighten his horse's girths, when Waters also obligingly pulled up his horse, apparently to wait for him; but at the same time, turning his mare's head toward the large wood which skirted the road, he

3. Of the Guards; afterwards General Sir Richard Jackson, Commander-in-Chief in Canada.
4. Many years after, this mare was turned out to grass by the Duke of Wellington in Strathfieldsaye Park, where she died and was buried

plunged the spurs in his steed's side. She bounded forward, clearing all difficulties, and in the full gallop of a well-bred English hunter, bade *adieu* to all followers and defiance to all obstacles: although instant chase was given, and shots fired after the fugitive, he gained the wood, adroitly threaded its intricacies, and escaped in broad day from his cavalry escort and the columns of French infantry! In a week after his capture, he presented himself once more at head-quarters.

On seeing Waters, Lord Wellington remarked, "Ah! I said so; they might catch him, but I knew they would not keep him." But to return: by some blunder of a staff officer, the attack on the enemy this morning was made too soon, none of the divisions of the army having reached their destined points; it ended however in the defeat of the enemy, by the gallantry of the Light and Third Divisions passing the river, and forcing them to retire. This was a very sharp affair; our two divisions, the First and Seventh, took no share in it, but were planted for three hours with piled arms in ploughed ground, and in heavy rain, hearing (for it was too thick weather to see anything) the rattling fire sustained at no great distance. The affair lasted only an hour, but Lord Wellington said that this was one of the most glorious actions the British troops were ever engaged in.

In this affair my poor friend Gurwood was severely wounded. After waiting thus unpleasantly and provokingly, we at length moved four leagues to our left, and got under cover at Angira de St. Antonio, a village more sonorous in name than accommodating in size; however, we were under shelter, and five of us, including the A. Q. M. General of the division, were stowed away, or confined, in a space about the size, colour, and appearance of a respectably-proportioned coal-hole in the neighbourhood of Berkeley-square.

Next day, the 4th, we halted in our delectable abode, having passed the night in as close relation to the poor inhabitants as sealing-wax to a letter; the worst was, that these inhabitants had inhabitants, who would not keep their distance, maugre our all lying in our clothes: it rained too hard to bivouac, and we could not conveniently cut off the communication of our too great proximity. Many sage and useful reflections suggested themselves to us, as to the advantage individually gained by young men travelling thus to see the world, and the knowledge of facts obtained by riding and walking through a new and wild country, without too frequently inhabiting houses, sleeping in beds, injuring our digestion by repletion, etc.

After all, we were the best disciples of Epicurus, for the true way to know the value of anything is to feel its want: the contrast from rough to smooth being transcendent, the enjoyment was in proportion. We had been able to calculate to a nicety the difference between the burning rays of a southern sun, and the winter bivouac among snowy mountains; between food and its want, thirst without beverage, and fatigue without rest; so we made ourselves happy, smiled at good fortune, and grinned and bore the bad; and, in opposition to every rule of arithmetic and calculation, made by the most celebrated actuary of the most respectable life assurance company, still persevered in the desire and intention to engage and beat the enemy wherever they might give us an opportunity.

The Peace Association might possibly consider these dark reflections from a coal-hole, but they were the best we could make from such an abode; and we hope for forgiveness, in consideration of the real love we had for our country, and the ardent desire we had to serve it disinterestedly.

On the 5th, as our brigade formed column to march, a dragoon of the First German Hussars brought forth a beautiful mare, which he was leading with one hand, while in the other he held his pistol; she moved with difficulty on three legs; the fine creature had, the day before, received a musket-shot in her fetlock joint; the wound was incurable, and she was condemned by the veterinary surgeon to be shot. The hussar informed us that, by her dexterity and speed, the poor animal had more than once saved him from death or a prison in France; and as he spoke of her merits, the tears ran down his hardened, weather-beaten and *moustachioed* face.

He conducted his fated charger to the rear of our column; we saw that once or twice the poor fellow raised the loaded pistol to the creature's head, and then, looking sadly at her, took it down again. At length, in an agony of grief, he dashed the pistol to the ground, and covering his face with his hands, wept aloud! He could not perform his duty, which one of our men was obliged to accomplish for him.

We moved from Angira de St. Antonio, passed the Coa, through Sabugal, and over part of the ground on which the action of the 3rd took place, to a village called Navé. Next day we marched to Aldea Velha, and as our column, soon after daybreak, was moving through the town of Alfyates, we saw Lord Wellington, who had apparently just risen, and was lounging out of window, looking gaily at us as we passed. He seemed in high spirits and well pleased, as well he might be; for the previous action at Sabugal had driven the last Frenchman out of Portugal, with the exception only of the garrison of Almeida and such as were his prisoners.

Thus gloriously and satisfactorily were vindicated Lord Wellington's views, and his capability of defending Portugal. This defence, long planned and well digested, was now effectually executed; a large party in the English Cabinet had been strongly averse to the undertaking, and I cannot do better than show, from the best authority, in what way and by whose decision Wellington and his army were allowed to save Portugal and to remain in the Peninsula.

Many years after the war, I was dining with Lord Maryborough, when he related that his brother, the Duke of Wellington, communicated in detail to the Government his plan for the defence of Portugal. These proposals were laid before the cabinet. It so happened, that the ministers were nearly divided in opinion, and came to no decision on the subject. Eventually however they agreed to submit the question to the King in Council, although the Prime Minister, Mr. Percival, did not incline to a continuation of the Peninsular war. When the King was informed of the circumstances, he determined this important matter in the following concise manner:

> Eh! what, what! Lord Wellington is a very obstinate man,—I suppose he must have his way.

In these few words was decided one of the most serious and eventful questions in the policy of our country; for it determined not only the fate of England, but it had a most powerful effect on that of all Europe. It was only one year after this that the poor old King was placed in confinement; at the time, his Majesty at least showed more sense than about one-half of his cabinet. Later,—however previously they had opposed or subsequently ill-supported these measures,—the dissentients took credit to themselves for the successful result, and willingly would have had the nation believe that it was "all their own thunder."

Secret expeditions, descents for inadequate objects on unhealthy coasts in the worst possible season, were more congenial to the understanding of such would-be statesmen. Had the troops sent to Walcheren reinforced Lord Wellington in Portugal, the saving of life would have been great, the expense not greater, and the result quite different.

All these miscarriages in our military policy at a critical moment in an eventful war, were engendered by the idea of creating a "diversion" in favour of somebody. Our Government certainly succeeded, as most people laughed, except those who caught the Walcheren fever. Lord Porchester's[5] motion in the Commons for "inquiry into the origin and conduct of this expedition to our opposite coasts," sufficiently showed, as far as the "origin" went, the prevailing excesses of small minds in great places; and as to the "conduct of the expedition," the well-known lines—

> *The Earl of Chatham, with his sword drawn,*
> *Stood waiting for Sir Richard Strachan;*
> *Sir Richard Strachan, 'longing to be at 'em,'*
> *Stood waiting—for the Earl of Chatham,—*

leave no further description of this melancholy history nec-

---

5. Lord Porchester, afterwards second Earl of Carnarvon.

essary.

From Aldea Velha we moved on to Forcalhos (a frontier village of Portugal). Here we experienced very cold weather, with a fall of snow. Out of thirteen horses and mules belonging to different officers, and enclosed for the night in one yard, some thrifty fellow, of more good taste than morality, stole the two mules I had purchased of Lord March just before we moved from Cartaxo. However much, on some occasions, it is desirable to be an object of preference, I could have dispensed with the advantage now; and had I been acquainted with Oriental sayings in those days, I should have expressed a wish that the purloiner of my mules might for ever have "a jackass sit on his grave."

A year after I discovered that the culprit was a Spanish muleteer, and I recovered one of the animals. My loss in horse and mule flesh since my arrival in Portugal amounted to one hundred pounds, besides the risk, on this occasion, of being obliged to leave my baggage behind—an inconvenient idea to reflect on. However, by the obliging assistance of our battalion surgeon and the commissary of our division, it was conveyed till I could provide myself with fresh beasts of burden.

On the 9th we entered Spain, and occupied the frontier village of Almadilla. A brother sub. and I were quartered in the entrance-room of a cottage, which served for parlour, kitchen, and all; we were doubled up with the inhabitants, six or seven poor Spaniards, who were cooking and eating, at various hours of the day, a mixture of oil, cabbage, and garlic, with a small piece of hog's flesh. An earthen pot (called a *pinetta*) containing this mess was constantly simmering over a small fire of damp straw and a few sticks. When wanted, it was turned out into a large earthen dish placed on a stool; when the partakers, sitting around on the floor, or on low three-legged seats, drew out their long knives from their waistbands, and proceeded to business with much solemnity and good breeding, without any appearance of hurry or too great an appetite.

One of them would commence by cutting slices from the large loaves of their most excellent bread (the sight of which was a novel luxury for us to look upon); and after distributing these, they dipped their bread, knives, and fingers into this garlic-smelling mixture, and bobbed for the morsel of bacon, on catching which each contented himself by rubbing it on the bread, and then returning it into the dish. In this common hall for cooking, eating, sleeping, and exit to the street, there was no chimney; the smoke escaped by a few tiles removed from the roof, which by no means sufficiently answered the purpose; the consequence was, that our eyes and organs of respiration suffered considerably. It did not however affect these poor people, who seemed, like their own bacon, to be smoke-dried. As it may be supposed, we fed not with them, but cooked our own rations in our own way and at our own time.

We were much struck at finding, that whatever atrocities the enemy had committed on the towns, villages, and people of Portugal (encouraged as they were by their chief), their conduct was quite altered on entering Spain. We found everything here in a tolerably good state, the enemy having resumed their sense of discipline,—a point by far the most difficult to return to when once abandoned. This change was as sudden as it was remarkable. In our army Lord Wellington's severity and discipline originated as much in a feeling of humanity as that of the love of order and justice. He used to introduce everywhere the idea of duty, into small as well as great things, and instilled these principles throughout his army. When later he entered France, he wrote:

I will not have the French peasants plundered.

And again on another occasion he says:

I do not mind commanding a large or small army, but, large or small, it must obey me, and, above all, it must not plunder.

Lord Wellington now invested Almeida, and it was thought that it would not hold out for want of provisions. Massena fell back to Salamanca, on Marshal Bessières' Army of the North:

our chief went southwards, to superintend the operations of Marshal Beresford's corps. Now that Portugal had been freed of the enemy, the great object of the war was to maintain it so. The next important point was the possession of Almeida; after this, to be able to take the initiative, and carry the fortresses of Badajoz and Ciudad Rodrigo from the enemy. These frontier strongholds, once gained, would prove an obstruction to any future attempts of the French on Portugal, while it would give us every facility for a forward movement into Spain.

In spite of Lord Wellington's signal success, through good and evil report or estimation, still he could not, even at this time, depend on support from the English Ministry. The Opposition too, understanding as little as the Government of the nature or necessities of the war in which the country was embarked, gave loud vent to their discontent. Certainly the expenses were onerous, but the necessity was undoubted: some field was wanting on which to make a substantial war, and it was found in Portugal,—not by the foresight of English statesmen, but by the forecast and abilities of an English soldier.

People in England really understand very little or nothing about military matters. They are very patriotic, energetic, admire brilliant actions, and exact success; but, in the manner or means of attaining such a result, or the strategy and tactics necessary to accomplish it, they are as simple-minded as people not bred to the trade can well be.

Macaulay, in his essay on Hallam's *Constitutional History* says:

The jealousy with which the oligarchy of Venice and the States of Holland regarded their generals and armies induced them perpetually to interfere in matters of which they were incompetent to judge.

This was very applicable to England and its statesmen of the years 1810 and 1811. The people at this time were led to believe that Lord Wellington and his army were "in a scrape." This idea was engendered about the time of our retreat to the "lines," of the surrender of Badajoz, and was even continued long after.

It is reported that a Spanish officer of distinction said to Lord Wellington, in allusion to these adverse circumstances, "Why, this is enough to put you into a fever."

He quietly answered, "I have acted to the best of my judgement, and care neither for the enemy before me nor anything they may say at home."

The truth was, with the exception of the expedition to Egypt,—which was something more resembling a substantive war,— our good Government had always been employing small expeditions on partisan principles, with great supposed *secrecy*; in short, making little wars at great expense, and small imbecile descents on the coast of an enemy or supposed ally.

Paisley's *Military Policy of Great Britain* was not published till the year 1808-9, and was soon out of print. A second volume, promised and announced, never made its appearance; but, after that badly conceived, and worse executed, expedition to Walcheren, we had no more of these "secret little wars." Whether this was the result of their bad success, Lord Wellington's exemplification of good success, or Paisley's book enlightening the stupid, is difficult to determine; but certain it was, we had no more of that which was poetically alluded to in a famous song of the well-known Captain Morris:—

*I sing of Holland's gin;*
*Not the gin that Dutchmen trade in,*
*But I sing of the gin*
*They catch men in*
*Who go about crusading.*

On the return of the late Duke of York from one of those Dutch expeditions, he was on his arrival visited by Sir T. S———, one of his household, a well-known character; who, after congratulating his Royal Highness on his good looks and his safe return, said, "And I still further congratulate the country in not having had to ransom you."

The English Government, when it threw an army into Portugal, little fancied that it was about to change the face of the world. All this was due to Wellington; for, ill supported as he was, and with inadequate means, he created an army, and knew how to use it. In a corner of Europe, alone and in silence, he began operations which, by his success, and the example he gave to other nations, resulted in the overthrow of the French empire. He himself said, at Toulouse, on the conclusion of this war, that he "had an army that was ready to go anywhere or do anything."

We were now left, during the absence of Lord Wellington in the Alemtejo, under his second in command, Sir Brent Spencer, a zealous, gallant officer, without any great military genius; anxious and fidgety when there was nothing to do, but, once under fire, looking like a philosopher solving a .problem, perfectly cool and self-possessed, which befriended the exercise of his best abilities.

Our army was cantoned along the sources of the Azava and the river Dos Casas; the Light Division at Galegos and Espeja. For ease, our cantonments were extended; and we were sent on the 17th of April from Almadilla to Puebla de Azava, a better village, affording more room. Here we began to remark the superiority in appearance of the Spanish over the Portuguese peasants.

These Spaniards certainly were anything but good soldiers, but they undoubtedly possessed all the attributes to render them so. The peasantry are capable, on small nutriment, of supporting great fatigue; they are long-enduring and hardy, with no want of courage, and only require to be well officered and well organized. The Portuguese, without the same amount of these desirable qualities, made much better troops; and thus proved what may be done by the advantages of discipline.

They, poor creatures, were at this time suffering next to starvation in their ranks (so ill supplied were they, that on one occasion, on Massena's retreat, they were left for four days without food!) by the misconduct of their own Government, who, with combined ignorance, laziness, and roguery, left their own army in the last necessities, in hopes, perhaps, that we should take the burden on ourselves; and partially we were forced to do so. At Puebla we were constantly kept on the *qui vive,* in readiness to march at the shortest warning; and on the 27th of April moved again to our left, and returned to Almadilla.

Hearing that Massena and Marshal Bessières' forces had united, and were in motion again toward the Portuguese frontier, Lord Wellington left the Alemtejo, and arrived with us again; on the 30th of April, accompanied by Sir Brent Spencer, Picton, and his staff, he came to Almadilla, and returned shortly after to head-quarters at Villa Formosa.

Massena, having collected his army in the neighbourhood of Ciudad Rodrigo, was only waiting for the subsiding of the waters of the Agueda to pass that river and advance. A sudden order reached us on the 2nd of May, and we commenced a night march by the light of a lovely moon; our movement was directed on Navé d'Aver, to close on the rest of our army there assembling.

As soon as we sniffed the morning breeze, and the early summer dawn broke, we began to examine our neighbourhood and reconnoitre our neighbours: we found, at no great distance, plenty of friends, which was pleasant, as we knew that we had a much greater number of enemies in our vicinity. The French army under Massena recrossed the Agueda on the 2nd of May, with the view of relieving the garrison of Almeida. To prevent this, Lord Wellington concentrated his army in position on some gently rising but extensively open ground, above and in rear of the village of Fuentes d'Oñor. On the same day the Cavalry and Light Division, after a skirmish with the enemy, retired from Gallegos and Espeja on the Dos Casas.

On the morning of the 3rd, the First and Third Divisions took up a position at about a cannon's shot distance, in rear of the pretty village of Fuentes d'Oñor, and we lined some stone walls. About nine a.m. the enemy's force was discernible; and shortly after they commenced a cannonade on our left, and an attack on the village, which was gallantly defended by the light troops of the Third Division under Lieutenant-Colonel Williams[6] of the 60th, and the Light Infantry of the Third Division, supported by Dick of the 42nd, the Light Infantry of the 92nd, and the 5th battalion German Legion belonging to our division[7]. At two p.m. we moved to out left by a road leading to the rear. At a little before five, our division reinforced the Third with the 24th, 71st, and 79th Regiments, and were sharply engaged in the town and among the stone walls around it, contesting every inch of the ground.

This affair ended only at dusk, with the village still remaining in our possession. We lay on our arms all night, and stood to them an hour before daylight, expecting, by break of dawn, not "coffee and pistols for two," but cannon and musketry for 32,000 infantry, 1200 cavalry, and forty-two guns of the allied arms; whilst our opponents furnished 40,000 infantry, 5000 cavalry, and thirty pieces of artillery. But, instead of attacking us on the 4th of May, they seemed as pacifically inclined as Quakers, or as the Peace Society now are when in council assembled at Exeter Hall.

Thus the early morning passed; the heat of the day approached, with all its Spanish intensity; we lay on a dusty, sandy plain, unshaded and unshaved; the summer furnace of a southern temperature was, as the sun declined, succeeded by a beautiful calm evening; the gentle slope of our position (dipping down to the Dos Casas and the village of Fuentes, and rising on the other side toward that of the enemy) formed a kind of ravine, the bottom of which was of a rocky nature and divided the two armies, the outposts of each lining the banks of the little river. The enemy's main force occupied a plateau of rising ground on one side of this ravine, as ours did of the other. From our position we could plainly see all that passed in theirs.

In the cool of the evening a parade took place of the cavalry and infantry of the Imperial Guard. In their rear and on their left flank were considerable woods of cork-trees and of the ilex or southern oak; in front of these our enemy stood out in strong

---

6. Afterwards Sir William Williams.
7. Dick of the 42nd, afterwards Major-General Sir Robert Dick, killed at Sobraon.

relief and martial array, their bands playing as they passed in review before Marshals Massena and Bessières. It was a noble sight to behold within our reach these armed men, our nation's foe, surrounded by "all the pomp and circumstance of war," and induced the

*Stern joy that warriors feel*
*In foemen worthy of their steel*

On our side we had no reviews; the bands of the German Legion (belonging to our division) raised their strains in answer to the French, and gave back note for note, as on the morrow we did shot for shot. The moon rose, the bivouac fires were trimmed, the cigar smoked, and our soldiers sank to rest.

On the 5th, long before day broke, we were to be found in our ranks, arms in hand, anxious for some exploit, and ready for any necessity. Mute and still, we rested in expectation of daylight and what it might bring. The cold previous to early dawn seems in adverse ratio to the intense and broiling heat of the day; the dew in these latitudes falls heavy after sunset, and the chilliness is greatest at the point most distant from the previous day, and immediately before the dawn of the next. We stood shivering and anxious, quite longing for light, and heat, and movement.

Movement came before daylight, for I was ordered to join a detachment sent to reinforce the piquets of our brigade on outpost duty. The chief of our Division accompanied this detachment; and, as we arrived at the point of ground destined for us, dawn began to break. At some eighty yards' distance, and immediately between the enemy's *vedettes* and our own, we saw two French horsemen advancing on our sentries, one of whom turned round and gesticulated to the enemy in an incomprehensible manner, then again moved toward them, but at last directed their course toward us.

Sir Brent Spencer ordered one of our sentries to fire, which he did with good effect, and brought down the cavalier; while the other fellow galloped into our lines in no small alarm. We then found that they belonged to Don Julian Sanchez' guerrilla corps, who, not long previously, had taken a convoy of French clothing, and had bedizened themselves out in these false colours. This valiant gesticulator was Don Julian Sanchez' own lieutenant, who, by some mistake, in the dark had ridden between our piquets and those of the enemy: seeing himself so near the foe and so well backed by our infantry, in bravado he began to play antics and defy them, and us also, as we thought.

This folly cost him his life. Sir Brent Spencer was greatly annoyed at the mistake, as it occurred in consequence of his own order. Lord Wellington came down to the outposts; and the chief of our division, in making his report, expressed his deep regret at the occurrence. Lord Wellington, seeing it was a case for which there was no remedy, said, "Never mind, Spencer; it is only a Spaniard!"

Don Julian however was furious, although it was entirely the fault of the lieutenant; who had no business to be where we found him, or in the uniform which occasioned the unhappy error. Soon after this we were recalled, and rejoined our brigade on the summit of the plateau, where we had passed the night and still remained. The enemy, in the early part of the morning of the 5th, were quiet; but an hour or two after daylight, they moved some heavy columns and the greater part of the cavalry to their left. We broke into columns, and made a parallel movement along our heights to our right.

About nine o'clock a.m. of this sultry morning they commenced a heavy cannonade on us from their left and centre. On reaching the gently-rising ground, eventually destined for our part of the position, we witnessed a brilliant and animating sight. Looking toward our right flank, across a plain terminated by the thick cork wood, we beheld dense masses of men engaged in strife, and enveloped in dust and smoke.

At first, little was clearly discernible; by degrees however, coming out from this confusion, were developed forms and shapes—horsemen charging—artillery, with their horses at full speed, thundering forward with an *impetus* that forced a way through the enemy—and the Light and Seventh Divisions coming forth from the chaos, and coolly retiring *en échelon* of squares, exposed alternately to the fire of the enemy's guns and the menaces of their cavalry, which were met and checked by our numerically weak squadrons.

Here Brotherton of the 14th particularly distinguished himself; and the present Lord Londonderry[8] (then General Charles Stewart) took Colonel La Motte, of the 13th Chasseurs, in single combat, by dragging him by the neck from off his horse. In this *mêlée* Felton Hervey of the 14th, who had previously lost his right arm at Oporto, was ridden at by a French officer of the 13th Chasseurs à Cheval, who raised his sword to cut him down; when, perceiving that his enemy had but one arm, he dropped his weapon to the salute, and passed on!

George Fitzclarence also was wounded in this affair; but Ramsey of the artillery, by his prompt skill and intrepidity, saved his guns, and at timely moments presented his enemies with their contents. The steady and soldier-like manner in which the Light and Seventh Divisions seemed to rise out of this apparently inextricable confusion, and the way they repulsed the enemy's efforts, were really most admirable.

At this moment an incident which befell our *Chasseurs Britanniques* excited us much and added to the interest of the scene. They were in line when charged by French cavalry; their commander, Lieutenant-Colonel Eustace (now General Sir William Eustace), did not attempt to alter his position, but coolly received them in that formation. When within some fifty yards of his bayonets he poured in a murderous volley, which settled the difficulty, and induced those of the enemy left in their saddles to seek shelter in their rear from so rough a treatment. After this retrograde flank movement of the Light and Seventh Divisions, they were concentrated in rear and in support of our right.

The enemy's Second and Eighth Corps and their cavalry turned the wood and village of Poço Velho, which obliged Lord Wellington to throw back his right flank; the Seventh Division crossed the Turones, the Light Division retired over the plain,

8. He has died since this was written.

and the remainder of our division not detached, together with the Third and the Portuguese, withdrew to the rising ground we had previously occupied.

In consequence, our division held the right of the position. Eight of the enemy's guns were now advanced to within convenient range, and we soon began to feel the effects of the fire from these and their light troops. The guns of our division in our immediate front were commanded by Captain Lawson; they opened their fire with effect on the enemy, which, together with our Light Infantry and Rifles, covering our right flank (for we were *en potence*), and our piquets skirmishing in advance, guarded our front against any sudden predatory attack.

About this time Lord Wellington rode up; and seeing that the fire of the enemy's round shot, shells, and sharpshooters was beginning to tell on the front line of the division, he ordered us to lie down. There was an animated and cheery look about him as he gave the order, which announced his certainty of success, and strengthened our intention to carry it into effect. Our further orders were to remain on the ground until the enemy approached in columns to within some thirty yards, then to rise, fire a volley, and charge bayonets: but their masses of infantry never advanced.

A piquet of the Guards, skirmishing with the enemy, was attacked by cavalry, but resisted them with success. They were suddenly charged a second time from behind a rising ground, under cover of which the cavalry had approached unperceived. The horsemen dashed at once on them while in extended order, and took them in flank and rear, cut down the men in detail, and carried off many prisoners.

Out of a hundred rank and file and five officers, only thirty of the former and one of the latter escaped unwounded; one of the remaining three being killed and two taken. At this moment part of Lawson's guns under Lane opened with grape on the French cavalry and mowed them down, destroying, at the same time, many of our infantry, mixed up as they were in this *mêlée* with the French cavalry. Their reception from our guns being more

71

warm than pleasant, the enemy precipitately vanished. Many of the remainder of this piquet came in wounded; and Captain Hervey of the Coldstream, after resisting bravely, was cut down and ridden over, but escaped and rejoined his ranks[9].

The second officer who escaped was Captain Home of the Third Guards. He had a *rencontre* with three of the enemy's horsemen; in trying to take him one of them seized the string of a bottle hanging by his side, which broke, and the cavalry man carried it off as a prize; another grasped his epaulette, which was torn from his shoulder; and the third, finding he would not surrender, attempted to cut him down.

Home was a powerful man, and, although on foot, lunged with his sword and then closed with the trooper, seized him by the neck and attempted to drag him to the earth: the struggle was a fierce one, but the Frenchman, finding he was likely to be worsted, turned his horse sharp round and galloped off, leaving in the hand of his enemy his cross of the Legion of Honour, which Home brought back triumphantly to his corps. From Home's muscular appearance and well-known courage and determination he was very likely to have brought in both man and horse, had not the trooper made a timely escape.

The 42nd Highlanders, under Lord Blantyre, were also at the same time charged by cavalry, but gave the enemy no encouragement to make a second attempt on them. Here an anecdote was current of Captain Mellish, of sporting and Newmarket fame, and at the time in the adjutant-general's department. He came into the field that morning mounted on a very woebegone and sorry hack, a regular Rosinante, looking as if it had lived much too long on air and exercise.

Some ridicule was elicited by this turf hero and great judge of horseflesh possessing so curiously *infra dig.* a specimen of cattle: one said that Lord Wellington had sent for a pack of hounds, and advised him by no means to ride near the kennel; another suggested that it was unfortunate no knacker was to be heard of in the neighbourhood; a third offered him five shillings for his

9. This officer was afterwards killed at Burgos.

charger. Mellish took all in good humour, and said he would bet any man £10 that before the day was out he would get £25 for him. After some jeering the bet was taken.

The firing in the village of Fuentes being heavy, he availed himself of the first opportunity to convey an order there, and rode right into the thick of the musketry: his horse was shot under him: he claimed, as losing a second charger, value £25, and thus he won his bet. A severe struggle was now enacting at the foot and key of our position in the village of Fuentes. Here, among others, three battalions of our division were carrying on an intense combat with the enemy for its possession.

The 79th, or Cameronians, commanded by poor Cameron (who fell on this occasion), instead of covering themselves by the walls and houses, chose to stand on the top of the former, and were consequently knocked down very rapidly by the enemy. Cameron and other officers did their best to stop this most inartistical mode of carrying on such a warfare, but with little effect; as the Highlandmen exclaimed, "that they would rather stand at the top of a wall, and be shot like men, than hide behind it, and be killed like dogs."

The 24th and 79th, in contest with an enemy, were practising light infantry movements for the first time in their lives[10].

The 71st, under Cadogan, knew their work, were *au fait* at it, and consequently were useful to themselves and friends, and much more formidable to their enemies. After all, in our part of the position, we had but a tiresome day of it, being occupied in playing Wall to something harder than the enemy's Moonshine; for, notwithstanding our recumbent position, our line received plenty of fire, but returned not a single shot during the whole day. This was trying to the patience and worrying to the temper of our men. I may here venture to name a few trivial circumstances incidental to our situation, which may be explanatory to the peaceable, or of interest to the uninitiated in such scenes.

A man of our company fell fast asleep, and amused his com-

---

10. The folly of not accustoming our regiments at home to light infantry drill occasioned in this affair not only a great disadvantage, but the loss of many valuable lives.

rades much by snoring loudly: poor fellow! a cannon-shot fell on his neck, just between his head and his knapsack: instant death ensued, without consciousness, and probably without pain. His own particular friend and comrade immediately requested to have his shoes! Whether this was induced by affection for his friend, or the necessities of his feet, remains to this day unexplained. The whistling of a shell, and its striking amongst us, next occurred: the felt of a cap flew in the air.

Thinking, of course, that the cap and head had gone together, I turned to see who it was, when I beheld, amidst the titter and laughter of his comrades, the great, broad, good-humoured countenance of an Irishman named M'Culloch: he was sitting upright, a queer figure, with half his cap cut off close to his head. I asked him if he was hurt: the fellow replied, with a grin, "No, plase your honour; only a bit dizzy!" which answer amused the company, who seemed to take Mr. M'Culloch's escape for a good joke. (This poor fellow was only spared for a short time; during the subsequent siege of Ciudad Rodrigo he was crushed by the beam of a falling house.)

Many other men were harmed in various ways; and my inseparable companion, a favourite Portuguese dog, alarmed at the bursting of a shell near us, set up a loud cry, and disappeared never to return.

We next had an alarm of the approach of cavalry, and rose to receive them; but they changed their mind, and swept off to our left, and we once more sank behind the slight ridge which covered our front. We had scarcely however been a minute on our legs, when three of the men of oar company were knocked down. Shortly after a shell passed through the tumbril of one of our guns that was in action in our front, and in its transit lit a port-fire: the agility and rapidity with which the artillery-driver detached his horses from the shafts were admirable: he risked himself, but saved them.

The tumbril immediately after exploded, driving the splinters of the wheels, boxes, and shafts in all directions, by which some of our artillery were wounded. In the hollow in our rear, sinking toward the Turones River, was placed our support, belonging to the second line of our division, composed of part of General Howard's[11] brigade, the 92nd Highlanders, together with a brigade of the German Legion. All the missiles lighting on our heights, bounded on *en ricochet,* and fell among our reserve.

I remember one shot particularly, which, after striking close to our people, plumped amidst a group of staff and field officers assembled together in the bottom, taking off the head of General Howard's horse, traversing the carcase of that of his *aide-de-camp* Captain Battersby, carrying off the leg of Major Stewart of the 92nd, and, knocking down two rank and file of that regiment, went hopping on like a cricket-ball, as if it had done nothing,— although this shot may be . fairly said to have done its duty.

Felton Hervey, who in the morning had escaped from the sabre of the *preux chevalier* Frenchman, had, while riding in our front, another narrow escape toward the close of the day. A round shot struck his horse, and hitting his sabretash, traversed the animal's carcase; and passing between Hervey's legs, came out on the opposite side, close to his knee, inflicting on it a severe contusion, and throwing him, horse and all, to the ground, on the armless side of his body. He was much shaken and hurt, but would not leave the field.

As the enemy began to withdraw from before us, their fire slackened: their guns first retired, then their *tirailleurs* retreated, and we rose from our earthy bed to witness some beautiful practice from Lane's portion of Lawson's troop of artillery. To cover their retreat, some heavy columns of the enemy's cavalry advanced to within six or seven hundred yards, and began closing up, bent, no doubt, upon mischief, when Lane opened three guns on them with spherical case-shot: the practice was excellent, the shells bursting within a hundred to a hundred and fifty yards from the head of their columns, creating chasms in their ranks, destroying and rolling over horses and riders, and drilling openings in their masses as if cut down with scythes. The fourth shot sent them to the right about; and galloping off, they

11. Afterwards Lord Howard of Effingham.

escaped the storm of lead and iron from our guns.

This was the parting evening salvo; the enemy's fire with us ceased soon after five o'clock p.m.; in the village it lasted longer; but eventually the lower part of Fuentes was abandoned by both sides, our people holding the upper portion, and the enemy retiring to some distance from the little river Dos Casas, which now once more separated the two armies. The casualties in our brigade from a seven hours' cannonade and fire of musketry, including the killed, and wounded, and missing among the skirmishers, amounted to one hundred and thirty-six men and five officers.

This number would have been much greater had not Lord Wellington economized us by his order to lie down. In the field he was ever most chary of his men; following that sound principle of warfare which inflicts as much injury on, and receives as little from, an enemy, as the facilities of ground, the nature of a position, and the adaptation of his troops to it would allow. The general loss of the allied army in this action was 1500 men and officers killed, wounded, and missing; that of the French was considerably greater, besides their attempt to relieve their garrison in Almeida having been frustrated.

The sense of success was pleasing to us, and the greetings of the unharmed as sincere and cordial, as was our regret for those less fortunate than ourselves. Once more assembled round the bivouac fire, we began to think of the "creature comforts," which were not less acceptable from their scarcity; the piquets were thrown out, the moon rose, we wrapped our cloaks around us, and slept away the fatigue and heat of the day, many losing themselves in the happiest of all English soldiers' dreams—that of England, friends, and home.

# CHAPTER 5

# Battle of Albuera

The stars were still bright in the heavens, and the dawn of day from the east had not yet appeared, when we were again on foot, trying to descry through the dark some object that might lead to an idea of the enemy's further intentions. We saw nothing but their watch-fires, and all was in repose. As morning broke, our telescopes were in requisition: the enemy lay still before us—the day began its broiling course—the dead, and the carcases of horses, lay strewn about the field in front, where they had fallen.

A flag of truce was sent, and a mutual agreement come to that we should bury our dead. Brotherton carried the flag. He was requested by Hervey to seek out the chivalrous young French officer who had respected a disabled foe, by saluting instead of cutting him down, and present to him, in his name, a pair of English pistols which he always carried in his holsters.

On inquiry, it unfortunately was found that this gallant young Frenchman had fallen in the action of the previous day. During these few hours of civil intercourse, many of us, like school-boys released, rushed down to the Turones River to swim,—no slight luxury in hot weather, and in the absence of everything but one shirt, which, being washed, was left to dry on a rock, whilst we disported in the water. On this and the following day both armies remained in the same position. We were occupied in throwing up breastworks and making *trous de loup* in defence against their powerful cavalry.

On the 7th they made a reconnaissance on our right, to have a nearer view of these works. Very strong piquets were thrown out, and these were strengthened after dark. It happened, on the night of the 7th, that I was on outpost duty; Almeida was still held by the French, and, uncertain of Marshal Massena's intentions, Lord Wellington (who, the whole of this time, lay on the ground near us) exacted great alertness in the out-piquets, and an immediate report of the slightest movement in our front. About midnight I patrolled, in advance of our sentries, down to a *vedette* of the 1st Hanoverian Hussars. On communicating with him, he told me, in his own peculiar English, that "She move" (meaning the enemy).

I asked him his reason for thinking so; he answered, "Listen! you hear vagon and gun moves on de road." On placing my ear to the ground, I found this was the case.

I then asked in which direction he thought they were moving; he answered, "From de left to de right." I demanded why he thought so. "Because leetle ting (shadows) pass bivouac fire from der left to der right, so dey go dat vey."

Having, for my own satisfaction, ascertained the correctness of his intelligent observation, I reported the circumstance to my supporting piquet and the field-officer of the night. Lord Wellington immediately came down, and advancing to the outpost, asked, "Who reported that the enemy were in motion?" He was informed of the fact, as well as the grounds for the belief that they were moving in our front to their left. Lord Wellington reconnoitred himself, and being satisfied of the truth, said, in allusion to the Hussar's report, "A d—d sharp fellow that; I wish I had more of them." For the rest of the night Lord Wellington remained in his cloak on the high ground of the position in our rear.

In the morning we found that the enemy had withdrawn from immediately before us. On the 10th they repassed the Agueda, and withdrew altogether, moving on Salamanca, where Massena was relieved from the command of his army, and was succeeded by Marmont. Thus ended these movements, and the battle of Fuentes d'Onor.

The Duke has been accused of want of sympathy for individuals, and of having an insufficient sense of the services of his army. He certainly was not demonstrative; his habitual reserve often concealed feelings that he was chary of displaying; but he was always fair and just when circumstances did not involve a compromise of system, or interfere with his sense of the public advantage. In a letter of condolence to old General Cameron, on the death of his gallant son (who received his death-wound in command of the 79th), he says:

> I am convinced that you will credit the assurance which I give you, that I condole with you most sincerely upon this misfortune. You will always regret and lament his loss, I am convinced; but I hope you will derive some consolation from the reflection, that he fell in the performance of his duty, and at the head of your brave regiment, loved and respected by all who knew him, in an action in which, if possible, the British troops surpassed everything they had done before.

With regard to an insufficient sense of the services of his army, I will here relate an anecdote exemplifying his estimation of them, and characteristically truthful of himself and those he commanded. After the battle of Toulouse the Adjutant-General of Cavalry, Colonel Elley[1], dined at head-quarters.

The Duke was in unusually high spirits: he had received the announcement of Buonaparte's abdication; the war was at an end, and none seemed more rejoiced at its termination than the Duke himself. Sir John told me that he had never seen him in higher spirits or more communicative. The conversation turned on the late immediate movements of the two armies, when the

---

1. Lieutenant-Colonel Sir John Elley, of the Royal Horse Guards (Blue), entered that Regiment as a private soldier, served in the campaign in Holland under the Duke of York in that capacity, and afterwards as an officer on the Staff throughout the Peninsula and at Waterloo. By prudence, good conduct, sagacity, and courage, he mounted through every grade of the army to the rank of Lieutenant-General, K.C.B., and M.P. for Windsor.

Duke exclaimed, "I will tell you the difference between Soult and me: when he gets into a difficulty, his troops don't get him out of it; when I get into one, mine always do."

Looking on the action of Fuentes d'Oñor as an epoch which finished a particular period of the war on the northern frontier of Portugal, I may be allowed to indulge in some slight reflections on the French, our army, and the Portuguese Government. The enemy's conduct to Portugal had been not only foolishly faithless and unjust, but in every way most atrocious. Talleyrand said, in allusion to the commencement of the Peninsular war,

C'est le commencement de la fin;

and later, diplomatically observed,

C'est plus qu'un crime, c'est une faute.

However, the restless spirit of their resentment resembled virtue in one respect, as to do its work at a palpable loss, and thus to become its own reward. Individually, the French possess eminently good qualities[2]: it must be confessed that ,as a nation, although capable of good and great actions, they are often so trifling in serious matters, and so serious in trifling ones, that one never knows exactly when the sublime begins or the ridiculous ends. I do not coincide with an Hibernian friend of mine (a good hater, but whose hatred was tempered by the propensities of a bon vivant), who used to declare that, for his part, he would only "just lave enough of them alive to cook, and cultivate the vines!"

I differ from my friend sufficiently to be able to render them full justice. I know them to be a clever, intelligent, and agreeable people; and, in spite of their misconduct, we could not help admiring their powers of endurance, under every possible species and extremity of privation, and their continued gallantry and good humour under the most adverse circumstances. We were bound to acknowledge them a brave and worthy foe. No army

2. See the uncontrolled possession of Paris by the lowest rabble in 1830 for three whole days, without the slightest tendency to plunder, extortion, or violence, beyond the open contention with political adversaries.

but a French one could be capable of such a strain on order and discipline as to afford a nine months' sanction of marauding and laxity, and then rapidly at once to return to obedience and regularity.

Whatever virtues are possessed by an English army, woe be to the commander who relaxes discipline with them! The Duke's own orders and many living witnesses are sufficient to prove, that such liberties must not be taken with an army which, while under control, make the very best troops in Europe. The conduct of the Portuguese Government at this time was so tiresome, disheartening, and unjust toward their own army and their allies; their correspondence with Lord Wellington so prevaricating, imbecile, and dishonest; that we might well apply to our dear ally what Duke Cosmo of Florence said of his friends, "That we read in Scripture, we ought to forgive our enemies; but that we nowhere read, we ought to forgive our friends."

On the 11th of May, the enemy having recrossed the Agueda, with the exception of one brigade left in front of Ciudad Rodrigo, our army resumed its cantonments on the banks of the Azava and Agueda, and we returned to our former quarters at Puebla and Almadilla. Having been for ten days deprived of our baggage, which had been sent to the rear during the foregoing operations, it was no small luxury to be once more restored to servants, horses, clean linen, and razors.

The Sixth Division, after the action, resumed the blockade of Almeida; but, in spite of the defeat of the far superior force brought by Massena against Lord Wellington at Fuentes d'Oñor, and that by this result the relief of the French garrison of Almeida was for the time baffled, Lord Wellington, to his no small mortification, found that between the night of the 11th and the morning of the 12th the garrison of Almeida, after blowing up a portion of the works of the town, escaped.

This was occasioned by the dilatory compliance of a general officer with the orders he received from Lord Wellington; on their receipt, it was said that, instead of promulgating them immediately, the general put them into his pocket and forgot them.

The consequence was, that the troops destined to cover a point in the line between the Agueda and the fortress of Almeida, arrived too late to prevent their escape; and again, those who followed the flying garrison with inadequate force, attacked them (with more courage than prudence or military skill) when they had passed the river and had arrived within reach of support. Two divisions and a brigade had been left, to prevent the escape of 1400 men under Brennier; every necessary instruction was given by Lord Wellington, but all miscarried by the failure of a prompt obedience to orders.

In writing to Lord Liverpool, Lord Wellington says on this point:—

Possibly I have to reproach myself for not having been on the spot. However, it is that alone in the whole operation in which I have to reproach myself, as everything was done that could be done in the way of order and instruction. I certainty feel every day more and more the difficulty of the situation in which I am placed. I am obliged to be everywhere; and if absent from any operation, something goes wrong. It is to be hoped that the generals and other officers of the army will, at last, acquire that experience which will teach them that success can be attained only by attention to the most minute details, and by tracing every part of every operation from its origin to its conclusion, point by point, and ascertaining that the whole is understood by those who are to execute it.

Those who were witnesses of Lord Wellington's many difficulties, can attest that that of making the inattentive or incompetent comprehend his views and obey his orders, was not the slightest among them. No really good school, to form superior officers, had existed (India alone excepted). Since the days of Marlborough, no English army had been let loose on the continent of Europe to make substantial war; island generals,—half fish, half flesh,—with transports at their backs, like snails and their shells,—were employed to carry out some great effort of military strategy, begotten in the brain of some most unmilitary minister; "creating diversions," cutting Dutch sluices, or consigning men to die at unhealthy seasons in pestilential Flemish bogs.

One great minister, who shall be nameless, had a brother a general, to whom it was said he submitted all his plans; but as the minister was really a man of ability, although not military, and the other was a military man without any such advantage, the civilian, in imparting his military lucubrations to the soldier, did not reap the same benefit as Moliere did when he read his plays to his cook. All necessary requirements for so opposite and enlarged a game of war as was now to be played in the Peninsula, had to be created by the chief who commanded.

Commissariats, *depôts*, hospitals, transports, munitions of war, bullets, clothing, beef, gunpowder, and shoes, had to be conveyed, received, and distributed. All such details, at a distance from our naval resources, had to be thought of and provided for; and even down to the feeding and condition of cavalry horses, and the avoidance of sore backs, Lord Wellington had to remark and give instructions upon, besides the discipline of the army, the tactics of war, the cultivation of the good feeling of the natives, and the diplomatic relations with their Government.

He writes to Colonel Gordon, from Quinta de Granicha, June 12th, 1811:

> In addition to embarrassments of all descriptions, surrounding us on all sides, I have to contend with an ancient enmity between these two nations, which is more like that of cat and dog than anything else; of which no sense of common danger, or common interest, or anything, can get the better, even in individuals. Our transport, which is the great lever of the commissariat, is done principally, if not entirely, by Spanish muleteers; and, to oblige Mr. Kennedy, they would probably once or twice carry provisions to a Portuguese regiment; but they would prefer to quit us and attend the French, to being obliged to perform this duty constantly.

Lord Wellington had few to aid him in all this. With some bright exceptions, those sent out in the higher grades were anything but what was wanted, failing in all but personal courage. Like Lord Collingwood's supply of officers after the battle of Trafalgar, political interest, personal favour, and partiality outbalanced capability, activity, and fitness in those sent to fill up the vacancies created by death, wounds, or sickness. It was then from the junior ranks of the army that Lord Wellington made his officers: "the young ones," to use a sporting phrase, "will always beat the old ones," particularly when the last are without experience.

The young brigadiers, colonels, lieutenant-colonels, majors, and captains were those he looked to and made efficient; many, even of the last rank in staff situations, in the artillery and engineers, gained, by their intelligence, well-bought reputations for themselves, and often added to those above them approbation and honour which they did not always quite deserve, but which they accepted, being satisfied (however little their own promptness or discretion might have contributed to it) that success was the test of merit.

It was quite wonderful how the chief could work with such tools; and had he not created others of a sharper description to act as Mentors, failures and blunders would have been more frequent than they were. The most remarkable position of Lord Wellington was that in this army, which he continued to command for so long and with such brilliant success, he had not even the power of making a corporal: he might recommend for promotion officers who distinguished themselves, but that was not always attended to or complied with.

An instance of this, not a singular one I fear, was that of Ensign Dyas of the 51st Regiment, who twice volunteered to lead storming parties on the outwork of San Cristoval at the first siege of Badajoz in 1811. His name was mentioned in despatches, and Lord Wellington recommended him for promotion; yet he never obtained it till after the return of the army from the Peninsula in 1814, and then only by an accidental meeting with an influential person (the late Sir Frederick Ponsonby), who once more brought his services before the Horse Guards. Besides neglect or forgetfulness, there existed much jealousy of recommendations which interfered with home patronage.

Lord Wellington, writing in August 1810[3], to the then military secretary at the Horse Guards, Lieutenant-Colonel Torrens, remonstrates at the ill-success his recommendations met with, for promoting officers for services in the field. He says:

I have never been able to understand the principle on which the claims of gentlemen of family, fortune, and influence in the country, to promotion in the army, founded on their military conduct, character, and services, should be rejected, while the claims of others, no better founded on military pretensions, were invariably attended to. I, who command the largest British army that has been employed against the enemy for many years, and have upon my hands certainly the most extensive and difficult concern that was ever imposed upon any British officer, have not the power of making even a corporal!! It is impossible this system can last.

It will do very well for trifling expeditions and short services; but those who are to superintend the discipline, and to excite and regulate the exertions of the officers of the army during a long-continued service, must have the power of rewarding them by the only mode in which they can be rewarded,—that is, by promotion. I would also observe that this practice would be entirely consistent with the unvaried usage of the British army.

I must say, that the public can have no greater interest than in the conduct and discipline of an army employed against the enemy in the field; and I am thoroughly convinced that, whatever may be the result in my hands, a British army cannot be kept in the field for any length of time, unless the officers composing it have some hope that their exertions will certainly be rewarded by promotion; and

3. See *Selection of Wellington Despatches*, No. 425, by Gurwood.

that to be abroad on service, and to do their duty with zeal and intelligence, afford prospects of promotion not afforded by the mere presence of an officer with his regiment, and his bearing the King's commission for a certain number of years.

Our chief ends the above communication by saying,

I would not give one pin to have the disposal of every commission in the army.

It was the principle, for the public good, he advocated; not the patronage, that he desired to engross.

In creating the efficiency of his army against innumerable adverse circumstances,—disparaged at home, condemned by an influential portion of the press, contradicted by the Opposition, ill supported by the Ministry, and thwarted by our allies,—the devotion Lord Wellington displayed to his duty and to his country's interests, overcame all difficulties and vanquished all opposition.

This persevering and unwearied spirit of contention against obstacles, by its heartiness roused the self-esteem of others, and stimulated their faculties to aid and assist him in his objects. At the same time, no sacrifice of personal feeling on his part was too great to submit to, for what he deemed the public good; in proof of which I will quote a letter he wrote, on a previous occasion, to his brother the Marquis Wellesley, wherein he alludes to some disagreeable annoyances he had been subjected to by those in power.

"You will see," he says, "how much the resolution" (the cause of his annoyance) "will annoy me; but I never had much value for the public spirit of any man who does not sacrifice his private views and convenience when it is necessary."

In farther exemplification of how perfectly he acted up to this principle, it will only be necessary here to quote letters written at the time by persons in official situations (to be found in Napier's *Peninsular War*), which, together with his own despatches, demonstrate at once the ill support of all Lord Wellington's views by our own and all the Governments concerned, and his want of necessary means to carry them out; thus subjecting him, not only to the sacrifice of his private "views and convenience," but endangering the vital cause in which England, Portugal, and Spain were engaged.

Napier says:

The inefficient state of the English Cabinet may be judged of by the following extracts:—

*April,* 1810. I hope by next mail will be sent something more satisfactory and useful than we have yet done in the way of instructions. But I am afraid the late O. P. riots have occupied all the thoughts of our great men here, so as to make them, or at least some of them, forget more distant but not less interesting concerns.'

*April,* 1811. With respect to the evils you allude to, as arising from the inefficiency of the Portuguese Government, the people here are by no means so satisfied of their existence as you who are on the spot. Here we judge only of the results; the details we read over, but, being unable to remedy, forget them the next day; and in the meantime, be the tools you have to work with good or bad, so it is, that you have produced results so far beyond the most sanguine expectations entertained here by all who have not been in Portugal within the last eight months, that none inquire the causes which prevented more being done in a shorter time; of which indeed there seems to have been a great probability, if the Government would have stepped forward at an earlier period with one hand in their pockets, and in the other strong energetic declarations of the indispensable necessity of a change of measures and principles in the Government.'

*Sept.* 1811. I have done everything in my power to get people here to attend to their real interests in Portugal, and I have clamoured for money! money! money! in every office to which I have had access. To all my clamour and all my arguments I have invariably received the same answer, 'that the thing is impossible.' The Prince himself certainly appears to be *à la hauteur des circonstances,* and has expressed his determination to make every exertion to promote the good cause in the Peninsula.

Lord Wellesley has a perfect comprehension of the subject in its fullest extent, and is fully aware of the several measures which Great Britain ought and could adopt. But such is the state of parties, and such the condition of the present Government, that I really despair of witnessing any decided and adequate effort on our part to save the Peninsula. The present feeling appears to be, that we have done mighty things, and all that is in our power; that the rest must be left to all-bounteous Providence; and that, if we do not succeed, we must console ourselves by the reflection that Providence has not been so propitious to us as we deserved. This feeling, you must allow, is wonderfully moral and Christian-like; but still, nothing will be done until we have a more vigorous military system, and a Ministry capable of directing the resources of the nation to something nobler than a war of descents and embarkations.

A more perfect picture of an imbecile Administration could scarcely be exhibited; and it was not wonderful that Lord Wellington, oppressed with the folly of the Peninsular Governments, should have often resolved to relinquish a contest that was one of constant risks, difficulties, and cares, when he had no better support from England.

We remained in observation in the frontier villages of Spain, but the Third and Seventh Divisions were now ordered to the Alemtejo, to join Beresford, who was carrying on operations against Badajoz. Spencer was left in the north, in command of the First, Fifth, Sixth, and Light Divisions, and the cavalry.

On the 15th, Lord Wellington left us for the Alemtejo; but

before he reached it, the battle of Albuera had been fought. This action took place on the 16th of May. Soult having rapidly advanced from the south, in force, to raise the siege of Badajoz, Beresford met him at Albuera, and a bloody action ensued. Our people gained the victory in a brilliant manner, but this was not accomplished without considerable and severe loss.

Much more mischief would certainly have ensued had not Hardinge (now Lord Hardinge, commanding-in-chief the army, but then one of those young staff-officers to whom I have alluded) rendered timely and good service by his moral as well as personal courage, taking upon himself that day a responsibility of no ordinary kind, which mainly contributed to the successful result of the action. Lord Wellington writes as follows to Spencer, from Elvas, under date of the 22nd May:—

> I went yesterday to Albuera, and saw the field of battle. We had a very good position, and I think should have gained a complete victory in it, without any material loss, if the Spaniards could have manoeuvred, but unfortunately they cannot. The French are retiring, but I do not think it clear that they are going beyond the Sierra Morena. As I know you have plenty of correspondents, I do not give you any details of the action here, or of our loss.

Lord Wellington, writing to Admiral Berkeley, under date of May 20th, says:—

> The fighting was desperate, and the loss of the British has been very severe; but, adverting to the nature of the contest, and the manner in which they held their ground against all the efforts the whole French army could make against them, notwithstanding all the losses which they had sustained, I think this action one most glorious and honourable to the character of the troops.

After this action the siege of Badajoz was resumed under the same disadvantages with which it had been first commenced: insufficient material, no adequate battering train, inefficiency of implements, and tools of bad quality[4], no trained sappers and miners, a scarcity of ammunition, and great difficulty of transport. Everything immediately necessary to accompany or supply our army was conveyed on mule-back; the badness of the roads, the ill construction and scarcity of the Portuguese and Spanish bullock-cars, and the slowness of wheel-conveyance drawn by oxen in a mountainous country, rendering them less available and more cumbersome.

Another consideration was, the facility with which animals, carrying loads on their backs, can move on bye-paths, crossroads, and over the open country, disembarrassing easily the main communication when wanted for the operations of the army. (For this reason, in Belgium, previous to Waterloo, the Duke ordered all baggage to be conveyed as in Spain and Portugal.)

The interest of the war now turned toward the Alemtejo and the southern frontier of Portugal. We were still left, however, under Spencer in the north, to watch Marmont at Salamanca, the garrison of Ciudad Rodrigo, and some few outposts in the Agueda. One night I was on piquet: patrolling before daylight along a pathway in our woody and hilly neighbourhood, we perceived in the twilight two French soldiers on a marauding excursion from their own outposts.

Before they saw us we indulged in a slight detour, came suddenly on them, and made them both prisoners. One of these men told me that 20,000 of the enemy were moving from Salamanca, by the other side of the Sierra de Gatta, towards Badajoz. I sent my prisoners in, with this intelligence, to be further examined at head-quarters.

The next day Don Julian Sanchez came over to our quarters, and confirmed this fellow's story, that the enemy in front were moving. In consequence of this report, and what had occurred in the Alemtejo, Sir Brent Spencer deemed it necessary to move some of the divisions under his command to Lord Wellington's support, and ours was ordered to direct its line of march toward the south. This was considered so pressing and urgent, that we

---

4. The quality is not much better at present.

left Puebla on the 25th, at two o'clock p.m., and did not halt till one o'clock a.m. of the 26th, and then only until four a.m.

We reached Penamacor at six p.m. the same evening, having marched (through bad roads and over a mountainous country in the summer heats) fifty-six miles in twenty-seven hours, with only three hours' halt. On our arrival we found that we were not wanted in the south, but might be so in the north, and we received orders to march back again.

General Howard's brigade only, with the Portuguese, continued to move on to the Alemtejo, and we returned to Puebla, through Argira de San Antonio, Sabugal, Soita, Alfyates, Aldea de Ponte, and Almadilla. This was very pretty exercise, kept us in good wind and condition, and indulged us in the habit of stretching our legs; but it wore out that important part of a soldier's kit on service, the men's shoes.

Lord Wellington, who thought of everything, would scarcely have failed to communicate his wishes, had he wanted us. Certainly, Beresford's fighting at Albuera as he did was, to say the least of it, an inconvenient work of supererogation and a waste of life, which did not assist in any way Lord Wellington's plans. Badajoz could not have been taken with the inadequate means in our possession, and the defence of such operations was not worth a general action.

A timely withdrawal from the siege, without encountering the enemy, would have embarrassed Soult, economized our troops, and avoided a fearful risk, without the chance even of obtaining any adequate advantage. It is dangerous to trust with discretionary powers men who possess great courage and small perspicacity. Napier says,

> Practical study may make a good general, as to the handling of troops and the designing a campaign; but the ascendancy of spirit which leads the wise, while it controls the insolence of folly, is a rare gift of nature;

and even that, with all its influences, is not always successful in making others do right. But Lord Wellington, not having the attributes of Sir Boyle Roche's bird, "could not well be in two places at once;" he wrote however, after the battle, that

> the enemy never had such superiority of numbers opposed to the British troops as in this action.

One of our chief's greatest merits was, that the great " master never found fault with his tools." Whatever private strictures or intimations he might have made on mistakes, failures, and blunders, his public ones were never condemnatory. On all occasions, in this way, he displayed the utmost patience and forbearance to faults which required, from their consequences, the utmost exercise of these virtues.

Our return to the Spanish village, after our rapid run over the mountains at the back of the Serra d'Estrella, was greeted by the inhabitants with welcome and good feeling. Since we had been in Spain (the people finding that we paid for everything we wanted, and put them to as little inconvenience as we could help) our supplies and resources became more abundant, and our intercourse with the natives agreeable. They were a fine race to look upon, and much superior, in this respect, to their neighbours the Portuguese. Poor Portugal, desolated and ground down as it had been by the iron hand of aggressive war, did not at this period show in favourable contrast with the less oppressed Spaniards, about whom there was always a staid manner and a dignity of deportment very prepossessing.

On the 30th of May, being the birthday of his Spanish Majesty King Ferdinand the Seventh; a bull-fight and a ball, to which we were all invited, was given at Fuente Guinaldo by *Don* Julian Sanchez (formerly a respectable butcher in Ciudad Rodrigo) and the officers of his guerilla corps. Duty prevented me from availing myself of this opportunity to witness this truly national amusement; I heard however from my comrades, that much patriotism, with cold kid and fried fish, was displayed upon the occasion, and the annoyance created by one of our corps having killed Julian's lieutenant at Fuentes d'Oñor seemed forgotten.

The soothing influence exercised by the presence of many

pretty Spanish women softened all rude or contentious feelings or recollections. In return for this pleasant intercourse and hospitable treatment, we determined to give these ladies and the guerrillas a dance, on the 4th of June, the birthday of our own Sovereign.

There being no ball-rooms at the village of Puebla de Azava, we constructed a very pretty bower of leaves, lighted up with paper lamps, and wreathed round with flowers; the English colours formed an ornament at the upper end, or place of honour, of this temporary apartment; a band from the German Legion set the swimming dance in motion; we had waltzes, *boleros*, and *fandangos*, dark eyes, favourable glances, agreeable smiles, white teeth, charming figures, and graceful movement: We actually began to feel a little humanized; in short, to us it was *"una tierra de los duendes[5]."*

We were very attentive and careful in refreshing the sedentary *duennas*, those Cerberuses of young hearts, with ample portions of punch, wine, and cake, and with as good a cold supper as the facilities of the neighbourhood afforded. We even extracted from Ciudad Rodrigo (although in the enemy's keeping) many sweetmeats and *doñas hermosas*, to adorn our bower and deck our table.

All was in good keeping and good taste—gay, lively, animated, happy—when, about three o'clock in the morning, some fellow, of ill-omened voice and stentorian lungs, thrust his ugly warlike head through an aperture of our bower, and hallooed out, "March directly!"

Had a mine exploded among our peaceful, happy group, more sudden or greater confusion could not have been occasioned; hurry-scurry instantly ensued amidst officers, servants, guerrillas, and ladies; the latter cried out, *"Los Franceses! los Franceses!"* although we had very good reason to believe that they did not dread them half so much as their brothers and fathers,—that is, with the exception of the old ladies, whose nerves were more delicate than those of the younger portion of the sex.

5. Fairyland.

Then came a scrambling and inquiry among the servitors after plates, knives, forks, and spoons; the ladies and guerrillas calling for their horses; the drums beating the *générale,* men moving down to the company alarm-posts, batmen saddling mules and horses; in short, great excitement and more regret at leaving so suddenly many agreeable, but too recently made acquaintances; at last however, like good soldiers and light-hearted Christians, we submitted to the consolatory French maxim, "*C'est la fortune de la guerre.*"

Our column being formed, we moved on Almadilla, where we awaited further orders. No one about us seemed to understand what these movements meant, and if ignorance is bliss, we were left to its utmost enjoyment. At last intelligence reached us that the enemy, under Marmont, had made a show of passing the Agueda with some cavalry and a column of infantry. Sir Brent Spencer, brave as a lion in personal courage, was sensitively nervous in that moral portion of the virtue, the responsibility of command.

Much vacillation ensued. Brigadier-General Pack precipitately destroyed the recently repaired works at Almeida; our army was somewhat disjointed in relative connection to the different divisions; our movements seemed of an uncertain nature, and our baggage was somewhat widely dispersed over the country.

In this state the Adjutant-general Packenham observed that the French did not advance as if to give battle—that their numbers were small —their movements more ostentatious than vigorous, and probably designed to cover a flank movement by the passes leading to the Tagus. He therefore urged Spencer to assume a position of battle, and thus force the enemy to discover his numbers and intentions, or march at once to Lord Wellington's assistance.

His views were supported by Colonel Waters, who, having been close to the French, said they were too clean and well-dressed to have come off a long march, and must therefore be part of the garrison of Ciudad Rodrigo; he had also ascertained that a large body was pointing toward the passes[6].

At three o'clock a.m. of the morning of the 6th, we moved from Almadilla on Soita, where we again halted from eight till twelve. The whole of our *corps d'armée* was now in movement in three columns of divisions,—the First from Almadilla, Aldea de Ponte, and Villa Major; the Light from Espeja; the Fifth from Navé d'Aver, and Sixth from Almeida, Villa Formosa, and the surrounding villages, in full retreat toward the Coa. Some skirmishing and a cannonade ensued between the advance guard of the enemy and our Light Division and cavalry, in which Captain Purvis of the Royals distinguished himself.

In the night, as the Light Division, with their arms piled, were in bivouac, a sudden alarm took place in consequence of some fellow roaring out, "French cavalry!" There was no doubt that a charge was made on the sleeping troops, trampling over the men and their arms, hurting some of the former and knocking down the latter. On rising to seize their muskets, our people discovered a drove of some fifty unruly bullocks, who, led by one more hungry and adventurous than the rest, had departed from their line of march, trotted off from the roadway in search of food, and, in spite of their drivers, scampered over a part of the 43rd and 52nd Regiments.

In the confusion thus created, some fellow suddenly aroused from sleep, who had possibly dreamed of the enemy, seeing a dark body of galloping quadrupeds, called out, "French cavalry!" totally forgetting that outposts had been set to guard against such an unpleasant intrusion.

On the 7th we passed the Coa, and took up a position in its rear: there we remained till two o'clock p.m. of the 8th, when, Packenham and Waters's surmises of the intentions of the enemy proving correct—that their advance was meant to cover a flank movement,—and they having retired again, we received orders to march to Mimão, on the road to Penamacor, *en route* for the Alemtejo; thus keeping a parallel movement with Marmont's corps. The Light Division headed our march, leaving Penamacor

6. See *Napier*.

95

to our left.

Our movement was directed to the passage of the Tagus at Villa Velha by Pedragão, Escalhos de Ceima, Sarnardas, and Atalaya; the heat was something awful, particularly to our poor men, each of whom, under the weight of nearly seventy pounds[7] (including great-coat, blanket, knapsack, arms, and accoutrements), was moving, sometimes in the hottest part of the day, through deep valleys covered with the shrub of the gum-cistus, emitting a powerfully aromatic and sickening effluvium.

Thus surrounded and closed in by hills, the sun struck with intense force into these deep valleys, which, together with the dust raised by the movement of large columns of men, and a want of circulation of air, was most distressing and overpowering. I have seen a man's haversack wet with perspiration through his thick red coat, as if it had been dipped in water. Our men however bore this well, and few, if any, were left behind. One poor fellow was struck down by a *coup de soleil*.

After the first day or two, Sir Brent ordered us to march at one o'clock a.m., so as to reach our halting-place before the heats began. It is no joke to be exposed to the sun in Spain or Portugal in the middle of a summer's day, when the thermometer stands between 80° or 90° of Fahrenheit. When the enemy kept at a respectful distance, Lord Wellington always made us march in the night, so as to reach our bivouac or camp in the morning, before the sun's power prevailed.

On the 14th we passed the Tagus between two precipitous hills. The stream here is rapid, and its width more than a quarter of a mile; there were but two boats, each of which could transport only two hundred men at a time, so our transit was slow, and the passage of the guns and baggage slower. Poor Johnstone of the Artillery was drowned on this occasion; he was much esteemed by all, and looked upon as a fine fellow and good officer. Although young, he had served in the campaigns of 1808-9-10-11, and had escaped unharmed till now. Here, my cattle failing, I purchased another mule of Joyce of the 60th Rifles.

---

7. It is to be hoped that in future campaigns this load may be lightened.

On the 15th we bivouacked near Niza, and on the 16th reached Portalegre, refreshed by rain, which cooled us; and, after an absence from our baggage of two days, we entered our quarters, which comforted us. The siege of Badajoz had now been raised, and Lord Wellington wrote that:

> the quantity of 241b. shot, we understand, that could be sent from Lisbon was 480, which we fired in about two hours!

Picton said we had been "suing Badajoz *in formâ pauperis*"

Portalegre was, with the exception of Lisbon, the first entirely undamaged town that I had as yet seen since entering Portugal, and, consequently, the only one that gave any notion of the original national habits or peaceful employments of the people. It was a large well-built city, with the advantage of being neither dilapidated nor deserted, which was so far favourable as to give it (in comparison to what we had recently seen) a busy and somewhat thriving appearance. The Bishop's palace was a spacious building; the houses were good, with shops and other industrial indications of humanity.

The Light Division, being in advance of ours, reached it two days before us. General Craufurd, who was in command, took up his quarters at the Bishop's palace; Spencer, commanding-in-chief the whole of this wing of our army, sent on to take up his quarters in the said palace. His *aide-de-camp*, Captain Browne, found Craufurd in possession, and having announced Sir Brent's wishes, and his intention to occupy it, Craufurd, ill to manage and of fiery temper, did not like to vacate so comfortable an abode, and insinuated that he considered himself divested of military rank, and wished that his superior officer would consider himself so, and farther mentioned something about the possession of pistols, and other small matters concerning eight paces, which intimation he desired might be conveyed to Sir Brent, as a hint of the manner in which he meant to resist the intended ejection.

This was so strong a step against the rules of order and discipline, that Spencer was obliged to report it to Lord Wellington; and thus the chief had, among other more serious occupations of mind and time, to administer corrective advice to his fiery-dispositioned lieutenant.

Both Spencer and Craufurd were men of tried and well-known intrepidity, and such differences were ill-timed, foolish, and detrimental to the service. Certainly, on this occasion, the junior, to say the least of it, was rather too demonstrative of the want of estimation in which he held his senior.

Without vouching for its correctness, I may mention another anecdote of Craufurd, which was current at this time. He had some cause for discontent with a commissary attached to his division, who was displaced. On the appointment of another, the general formed his division into a square, and introduced the commissary; when, addressing his men, he animadverted on the misconduct of the former officer holding that position, who had not, he conceived, been sufficiently active in supplying the division; and added, that if the present commissary did not do his duty better, they might hang him, for what he cared!

This uncourteous announcement did not suit the commissioned dignity or personal feelings of the purveyor of provisions, who took the matter much to heart, and quite *au pied de la lettre*. Under this impression, and being perfectly unappeasable, he repaired to head-quarters, to make a formal report of what had occurred. Lord Wellington, happening at the time to be very much engaged, could not see him. He waited, and sent in a second time to say that he was in attendance. At last he was admitted; when Lord Wellington asked, "Well, what do you want?"

The unfortunate complainant, with much circumlocution, related his injuries. Lord Wellington could not bear a round-about story; conciseness, alacrity, and energy were the elements in which he lived. He liked all that was to be done or said brought to a point clearly and quickly; and when the commissary ended the history of his sorrows by saying that the general had declared "they might take me and hang me."

Lord Wellington replied, "Did he, by G——? You had better

take care; he is sure to be as good as his word."

On the 19th we left Portalegre, and it was with regret that we moved from so unusually good a quarter. Marmont, with the army of Portugal, directed his march by the Puerta de Bãnos, to join Soult. The whole French combined force of these two marshals, amounting to some 80,000 men, was now concentrated in our front. Lord Wellington writes from Elvas, under date of the 17th of June, 1811:—

> Under these circumstances I should, and shall, avoid a general action, if I can; but I must put a countenance upon the state of affairs, and matters must be risked till provisions be placed in Elvas.

With this view our chief visited the position of Albuera, and ordered entrenchments to be thrown up to strengthen this ground. Elvas, which had been perfectly neglected by the Portuguese Government (although their only stronghold of consequence in the Alemtejo), was now, at the oft-repeated demand of Lord Wellington, being provisioned and armed; and this at the eleventh hour. Some of the guns were so useless, and the ammunition so scant, that a detachment of French cavalry were allowed to pass over the glacis of the fortress without a single gun being brought to bear upon, or even a shot fired at them.

Our division on the 23rd moved from Azumar to St. Olaya, where we hutted ourselves. The same day:

> The French cavalry having passed the Guadiana in two columns, one by the bridge of Badajoz, the other by the fords below the confluence of the Caya; the former drove back the outposts, yet, being opposed by Madden's horsemen and the Heavy Dragoons, retired without being able to discover the position on that side. The other column, moving towards Villa Viciosa and-Elvas, cut off a squadron of the 11th Dragoons; and the Second German Hussars escaped from it to Elvas with great difficulty. One hundred and fifty men were killed or taken in this affair, and the French aver that Colonel Lallemand drew the British

cavalry into an ambuscade.

The rumours in the allied camp were discordant, but no more fighting occurred; and a fruitless attempt to surprise the English detachments at Albuquerque ended the demonstrations. The French marshals then spread their forces along the Guadiana from Xeres de los Cavalheiros to Montijo, and proceeded to collect provisions. A great and decisive battle had been expected; and though the crisis glided away quietly, the moment was one of the most dangerous of the whole war[8].

---

8. See Napier.

# CHAPTER 6

# Advance of the French

Lord Wellington wrote from the Quinta de San João under date of the 30th June:—

As nothing is believed in England that is written by persons in authority in this country, it is not believed that the generals commanding the French armies have no communication with each other, and that they are entirely ignorant of all that is passing around them; and that they have, in fact, no information, excepting what they derive from deserters from the foreign regiments in our service,—of whom there are, I am sorry to say, too many,—and from the prisoners occasionally sent back to them, in exchange for some of our officers and soldiers. Adverting to the superiority of the enemy's numbers over the allied British and Portuguese armies, and to the inefficiency of the Spanish troops, I attribute the success which we have had hitherto in a great degree to the want of information by the enemy's general officers. At this moment, though the whole army are within a few miles of them, they do not know where they are; but, if disabled prisoners are to be sent to them, they will get all the information they require, if not directly from themselves, from their friends in the French interest at Lisbon, from Portuguese or English newspapers etc.

And further to show the state of affairs at this period, it may be as well to quote other short extracts from a letter of Lord Wellington's to General Dumouriez, under date the 5th July, from the same *Quinta*.

*Il y a presque trois ans, à présent, que je conduis les opérations de la guerre la plus extraordinaire qu'il y eût jamais. . . . Je crois que ni Buonaparte, ni le monde, n'ont compté sur les difficultés à subjuguer la Péninsule, étant opposé par une bonne armée en Portugal. Il a fait des efforts gigantesques, dignes de sa réputation et des forces dont il a la disposition; mais il n'en a pas fait assez encore; et je crois que l'ancien dictum de Henri Quatre, que 'quand on fait la guerre en Espagne avec peu de monde, on est battu, et avec beaucoup de monde, on meurt de faim,' se trouvera vérifié de nos jours; et que Buonaparte ne pourra jamais nourrir, même de la manière Française moderne, une armée assez grande pour faire la conquête des royaumes de la Péninsule, si les alliés ont settlement une armée assez forte pour arretêr ses progres. . . . Vous verrez quelle est l'espèce de guerre que nous faisons. Il faut de la patience, de la grande patience, pour la faire, etc.*

We remained in our hutted camp in daily expectation of the enemy's movement in advance. The heat was excessive, our shelter from its in-tenseness inadequate; large plains, dotted and interspersed with olive-trees, afforded more dust than shade; our huts were not constructed of the best materials to defend us from the sun's scorching blaze; soon after daybreak they became little hot-houses, or rather ovens, from whence came forth for parade an almost baked battalion.

At this place our brigade was considerably strengthened, by a reinforcement of detachments from our different regiments at Cadiz. Here also his Royal Highness the Prince of Orange joined us, as *aide-de-camp* to Lord Wellington. He was accompanied by his friend, Henry Johnson[1], acting as his equerry and *aide-de-camp*.

On this occasion Lord Wellington reviewed the whole army, to show it to his Royal Highness. To be sure, we were not so

---

1. Now Sir Henry A. Johnson, Bart., of Gresford Lodge, Denbigh.

numerous as the combined corps of the two French marshals in our front; but what there was of us, together with the Germans, improved by past experience under Lord Wellington's guidance, was tried good stuff.

At the same time our ranks were a motley group of all nations, British, Hanoverians, Brunswickers, Chasseurs Britanniques (composed of French royalists and deserters), Portuguese, and Spaniards. We were in appearance like Joseph's many-coloured garment; whilst our enemy formed one compact army, under French chiefs, with the advantage of one discipline and one language. In our ranks sickness began now to prevail to a considerable extent. Our vicinity at this season to the banks of the Guadiana was anything but healthy: fever existed on the low and extensive plains surrounding the river. We were not sorry to find, therefore, that the enemy had withdrawn from before us.

After provisioning Badajoz, "Marmont covered Soult's retrograde operations and retired gradually; he quartered his army in the valley of the Tagus, leaving one division at Truxillo." We were thus relieved from the French when we had most reason to expect, if not an attack from them, at least one from the Guadiana fever. Indeed, the latter had already made some progress; but we were now spared a further contest with both, and the inconvenience of a longer residence in an unwholesome vicinity. Want of provisions and the pestilent neighbourhood induced the enemy to decamp.

Marmont so placed his force on the Tagus as to act on the flank of any movement of ours against Soult and towards Andalucia; his central position covered Madrid, and he could in a short time collect 70,000 men against any incursion Lord Wellington might have contemplated in that direction; but after ally the concentration by the two French Marshals of 80,000 men did not result in a renewal of an attempt to invade Portugal. We therefore regarded each other with contemplative curiosity, our chief waiting and watching like a tiger for a spring upon his prey.

On the 2nd of July we broke up from our camp, and marched,

*viâ* Azumar, to Portalegre. Here Lord March left head-quarters on sick leave for Lisbon, and Sir Brent Spencer left for England. The latter had frequently been good enough to notice me; and, on taking leave of him, he informed me that, in consequence of Sir Thomas Graham's appointment to this army as second in command (having held that high position himself for so long), he could not reconcile to his feelings to accept a lower post, such as remaining in command of the First Division, which had been offered him by Lord Wellington.

He had therefore determined to resign and return to England; that he mentioned this to me, as he had intended to have appointed me his *aide-de-camp*, had I liked to serve on his personal staff; and that, should he be employed elsewhere, he would keep the appointment open till he heard from me. I thanked him for his kind intentions, and the estimation in which he was good enough to hold me; and replied, that should he hold any command on active service, I would most readily accept his offer, but that in any other case I should be loath to leave this army, as I conceived it to be the duty of every young officer to serve where he could most profit in the knowledge of his profession. He was good enough to approve my views, and so we parted, and the matter ended; for he did not succeed to Sir George Prevost's command in America, as was at the time contemplated.

During the few days we halted at Portalegre, a young, gallant, and hilarious major-general (who was quartered in the Bishop's Palace, near the church) had, as usual, a few officers at dinner. The company was composed of youthful and buoyant spirits like himself; the weather was very hot, and the wine very plentiful. After a somewhat late sitting, it was proposed, in consequence of the tempting vicinity of a wardrobe full of canonicals, to attire ourselves in priestly garments, and to march forth with long candles in our hands; this was put into effect, chaunting, in grave procession, as we went, most unintelligible music, interrupted by bursts of laughter. Luckily, it was late and the inhabitants were at rest; or otherwise disagreeable consequences would in all probability have ensued.

A report of this effervescence of wine and reckless spirit reached head-quarters; and, considering the sacred ceremonies it imitated, the prejudices it waged war against, the high military rank of the person engaged in it, and the consequent bad example to others, this escapade was severely rebuked by Lord Wellington. He who was the promoter of the fun and folly will now perhaps smile as he recognizes the scene of past thoughtlessness (should its relation meet his sight), for he still lives[2]; and but lately, at St. Paul's, I saw him shed abundant tears of regret on the bier of him who recalled the too lively young general to a sense of his position. Thus was settled this great candle and surplice question, which unfortunately in these days cannot be so easily settled at home!

Lord Wellington then turned his mind to other cannons, not of the Church, but of those in the mouth of which "man seeks the bubble, reputation."

He caused the battering train of iron guns and mortars, just arrived from England, with their gunners, to be re-embarked ostentatiously at Lisbon as if for Cadiz, but had them shifted at sea into smaller craft; and while the original vessels went to their destination, the train was, secretly landed at Oporto, and carried up the Douro in boats to Lamego. From thence they were brought to Villaponte, near Celorico, without attracting attention; because Lamego and Celorico, being great *depôts*, the passage of stores was constant. Other combinations deceived the enemy and facilitated the project, before the troops commenced their march for Beira. The bringing sixty-eight huge guns, with proportionate stores, across fifty miles of mountain was an operation of magnitude. Five thousand draft bullocks were required for the train alone, and above a thousand militia were for several weeks employed merely to repair the road[3].

---

2. I am sorry to say that he has died since this was written.
3 *Napier.*

At about the same time all our field-guns, except those of the Horse Artillery, were exchanged for others sent out at Lord Wellington's request. We found the French eight-pounder guns overpowering against our sixes, nice light little things, fit only for short and sweet Lilliputian boating expeditions, but not made to contend with the heavier calibre of metal the enemy brought to bear upon us.

Lord Wellington, immediately after the battle of Albuera, had sent Beresford to Lisbon to organize the restoration of the Portuguese army. No man was more fit and capable for the execution of this object than Lord Beresford, as demonstrated by the organization, the discipline, and eventual state of the Portuguese army, which had hitherto been paid by England, and three-fourths of them supplied from our commissariat; but still the Portuguese Government left the remaining fourth to starve.

The disputes between Lord Wellington and the Portuguese Government were also becoming unappeasable; he drew up powerful expositions of his grievous situation, sent one to the Brazils, and another to England, declaring that if a new system was not adopted he could not and would not continue the war[4].

The successful results of the conduct of the campaigns in the Peninsula by Lord Wellington's prudence, activity, and foresight, seem at length to have inoculated the Ministry in England with more confidence in his views and somewhat less in their own. Luckily, at this moment no cabinet minister happened to be affected with that serious and cruel disorder, a strategic expeditionary mania to any other part of the new or old world; so we began to be more effectively supported with men and material, although money was still wanting in our military chest.

This change for the better did not occur till after the army had been engaged in this war for nearly three years; and, in spite of all the representations made by Lord Wellington, Mr. Percival still remained inimical to his views, and either would not or

4. Napier.

could not understand this great concentrated effort towards one grand and worthy end. The Spaniards would not consent to be officered by us; and at this moment were, as far as their armies went, really of little or no use.

Lord Wellington writes to his brother on this subject as follows:—

> You will then say, what is Great Britain to do? I answer, persevere in the contest, and do the best she can; while she endeavours to prevail upon the Spaniards to improve their military system. We have already, in some degree, altered the nature of the war, and of the French military system. They are now, in a great measure, on the defensive, and are carrying on a war of magazines. They will soon, if they have not already, come upon the resources of France; and as soon as that is the case, you may depend upon it the war will not last long.
>
> We may spend ten millions a year in this country, but it is a very erroneous notion to suppose that all that expense is incurred by the war in the Peninsula. Our establishment which we have here would cost very near half that sum if they were kept at home, and the surplus only should be charged as the expense of this war. I do not mean to say that that expense is not great, but it must be borne as long as the Spaniards and Portuguese can hold out, or we must take our leave of our character as a great country.

The military departments at home also seemed in happy ignorance of the nature of the requisites essential for an army established in continuous warlike operations on the continent of Europe. Pigtails, pipe-clay, stiff stocks, powder, tight breeches, long gaiters, and eight hundred lashes before breakfast, were the costume and discipline of that day and the old time before it. These antiquated notions began to be loosened, through the practical knowledge and necessities of the war.

We ourselves were in a normal school of education under him, who lived to see and assisted to make great and advantageous changes and improvements, Lord Wellington, having changed the artillery of the army to a larger calibre of gun, and received reinforcements of some cavalry and infantry from England, once more set us in motion for the north of Portugal, having obtained intelligence that Ciudad Rodrigo was straitened for provisions.

On the 31st, accordingly, our division moved from Portalegre to Alpahão; on the 1st reached Niza; and on the 2nd passed the Tagus on a pontoon bridge—another most requisite material for an army, and now for the first time only in our possession. In descending from the north, the flying bridge of two old crazy boats was the dilatory and only mode of transit over the Tagus. (Here, by moonlight, after so many hours' exposure to the sun, sundry of us took a most luxurious swim in the Tagus.)

On the 7th our new chief of division, Sir Thomas Graham[5], joined us as second in command of the army. He was a fine, gallant-looking old man, who began his military career somewhat late in life, by raising, at forty years of age, a regiment, of which he became at once the colonel, and in this rank commenced his services.

We continued to move by Sarnadas and Castello Branco to Escalhos de Ceima, where we had a day's halt; then on to San Miguel, Pedrogão, Val de Lobo, and finally to Penamacor, where we halted, The Light Division took up their old quarters between the Agueda and Dos Casas, at Gallegos and Espeja. Lord Wellington left General Hill with 10,000 men in the Alemtejo to watch Soult, and cover any attempt on Lisbon from that quarter; Hill's front being covered again with some Spanish corps. It was remarkable that he was the only one of his generals, after the battle of Albuera, to whom Lord Wellington confided, for any length of time, the command of a separate corps; and well did General Hill merit the confidence placed in him.

No man however was more fair and considerate towards a first failure of others in a military attempt than Lord Wellington. A staff-officer, attached to head-quarters, informed me he had

---

5. Afterwards Lord Lynedoch,

heard him declare that a man failing once (under certain circumstances) should not preclude his being tried again; and on one occasion he added, "Where should I have been had I not had a second trial at Seringapatam?"

Marmont was drawn to the north by our movements; and although our advance arrived too late to prevent some small supplies reaching Ciudad Rodrigo, still the enemy made no attempt to molest any of our corps on their march, except by some French dragoons from Plasencia, who "captured a convoy of mules loaded with wine, got drunk, and in that state falling on some Portuguese infantry, were beaten, and lost the mules again[6]."

On this march, the weather being very hot, most of us preferred bivouacking to sleeping in the filthy cottages, with their too numerous inhabitants. One of my horses knocked up, and I left him, poor fellow! on the top of a mountain, at his own discretion, to sustain himself as best he could on some sorry-looking leaves and grass.

I had no choice in the matter, or he either: he could not move further. It was no longer possible for him to carry me; and, as it did not occur to me to parry him, we parted, wishing each other well, no doubt. I lightened his back of the saddle, which I placed on my own till the day's march was over. Privations and hot weather render men anything but amiable.

It requires much forbearance and good feeling in such positions to "love your neighbour as yourself;" besides, perhaps the fiery sun may add to fiery tempers; for which reason there generally is more squabbling in India than elsewhere; in short, people get bilious, if they are not "born so." Heaven knows, as far as indulgence in comestibles went, we had neither profuseness nor luxury to generate dyspepsia.

But, be this as it might, it did not prevent two field-officers of our brigade from coming to loggerheads. One of them established himself at the village of Pedrogão, in some hovel, more convenient-looking than ordinary. The other, of senior rank, ar-

---

6. *General Harvey's Journal*, MS. See *Napier*.

rived later, but, on doing so, turned out the first possessor. Warm expressions passed in consequence; and the following day, while on the march, the ejected party rode up to, and remonstrated with, the ejector.

The latter coolly assured him that, "so far from relinquishing his right to what he had done now, he should continue to act in the same manner on all future occasions."

The other replied that, in such a case, he "sheltered himself under his rank as a superior officer, to be guilty of a dirty and ungentlemanlike action." This, of course, was a closer to the conversation at the time.

After some little delay, these two men went out; the junior fired at the senior, the senior at the junior, and so ended this stupid and ill-conditioned dispute. Most people thought that, as the French were so near, it was a pity these gentlemen should have had occasion to try to shoot one another; by only going a little distance the enemy would, in all probability, have done it for them with the greatest possible pleasure, and in a much more soldier-like and professional way.

Our subordinate rank precluded us from entering into the indulgence of such luxuries: we belonged to that happy portion of his Majesty's service who were in the full enjoyment of what sailors call "monkey's allowance," that is, of "more kicks than halfpence."

With the alacrity of youth, however, the necessity of obedience to those numerous grades above us, and the inutility of resistance, I do not remember any instance of a duel among the subalterns; although I have seen men turned out, not only of quarters, by those immediately above them in seniority, but even from under the scanty shade afforded by an olive-tree.

At that cheery age we bore all, laughed at all, and were ready for all. We left it to those of higher rank, and more matured ill-temper, of less good feeling, or absence of good breeding, to set so bad an example when on service before an enemy.

The English newspapers of the 15th July reached us here, and kindly communicated to us that we had all retired to our lines at Torres Vedras[7]!

On the 28th of August however we moved from Penamacor, and closed up to our advanced divisions on the frontier of Spain, passing through Val de Lobo, Sabugal, to Navé d'Aver. Ciudad Rodrigo was now surrounded by the piquets of the Light Division, which were extended to the Salamanca side of the town, cutting off the communication between the garrison and the surrounding country. Marmont was at Plasencia, and Dorsenne, with 20,000 men, in the north; their communication with each other was sustained through the passes of the Sierra de Francia, "where, early in September, Marmont pushed a detachment from Plasencia, and surprised a British cavalry piquet at St. Martin de Trabejo, and this opened his communications with Dorsenne."

Ciudad Rodrigo could not be besieged in the face of these combined corps, and even the blockade must be raised if they united and advanced. Our Spanish allies were at this moment of small, or rather, of no use to themselves or us. From the reports of reinforcements arriving to the French in Spain, the formation of depots at Burgos, etc., and, lastly, that Napoleon himself meant to head an army to drive us from Portugal, Lord Wellington was induced to order the lines on both banks of the Tagus around Lisbon to be again strengthened, and many additional labourers were employed in their further improvement and completion.

The garrison of Rodrigo now again became short of provisions; Marmont had been reinforced from France, and had

---

7. As illustrative of the ill-omened reports and opinions existing at home at this time, I may venture to quote an anecdote from *Moore's Diary*, with a note of Lord John Russell's on it.

"Sheridan always maintained that the Duke of Wellington would succeed in Portugal; General Tarleton the reverse. It was a matter of constant dispute between them. Tarleton, who had been wrong, grew obstinate; so on the news of the retreat of the French, Sheridan, by way of taunt, said, 'Well, Tarleton, are you on your high horse still?'—

'Oh, higher than ever! if I was on a horse before, I am now on an elephant.'—

'No, no, my dear fellow; you were on an ass before, and you are on a mule now.'"

Lord John goes on to say, "I remember that, having been at the lines of Torres Vedras, Sheridan was much pleased with my sanguine account of the position.—Ed. of *Moore's Letters and Diary*."

50,000 men. He now entered on a combined operation with Dorsenne, to succour the garrison of the above place. Marmont passed the mountains, and collected a large convoy at Bejar; Dorsenne and Souham collected another convoy at Salamanca, and came down to Tamames on the 21st.

This was a far superior force to any that we could front them with; and although Lord Wellington was unable to fight beyond the Agueda, he would not retreat till he had seen the French army, lest a detachment might relieve the place, instead of their being obliged to bring their whole force to effect that object.

The operations which followed Marmont's advance it is neither my province nor my intention to detail, further than to afford' some general idea of what occurred. In our extended position, covering the different roads and their wide range leading into Portugal, personal observation of simultaneous events, beyond our own immediate locality, was out of the question. I can only narrate, therefore, the occurrences to the different corps and to individuals, as they came to my knowledge after the events.

Marmont's specific object .was the maintenance of Ciudad Rodrigo, hitherto surrounded by our outposts, to regarrison it with fresh troops, and to supply it amply with food and military munitions. Situated as we were, this object could not be prevented, except at the risk of a general action against a superior force; which, having no sufficiently adequate object to attain, Lord Wellington did not contemplate.

On the 23rd the advance guard of the enemy's *corps d'armée* made their appearance from the hills, and descended into the plains surrounding the fortress, but they soon after withdrew. Our divisions were distributed as follows:—the Light Division at Vadillo, near Ciudad, well posted to watch the enemy's advance; the Third Division at El Bodon and Pastores, supported by the Fourth in the neighbourhood of Fuente Guinaldo, which place was Lord Wellington's head-quarters; the Sixth, with Anson's cavalry, at Espeja and Campillo; the First, Fifth, and Seventh being in reserve at Payo, Almadilla, and Navé d'Aver: the last was our post, where we were held in immediate readiness to support either our front, our right, or any divisions needing our collateral assistance. The baggage was despatched to our rear and to the other side of the Coa; our movements were thus left disembarrassed from encumbrances either in "highways or bye-ways."

On the 24th a corps, under General Montbrun, again advanced, and crossed the Agueda with 6000 cavalry, four divisions of infantry, and twelve guns. At daybreak on the 25th the enemy made a reconnaissance, to mask the introduction into Ciudad Rodrigo of their convoy of provisions and a fresh garrison. With this intention they passed the Lower Azava with fourteen squadrons of cavalry of the Imperial Guard, and with a *corps d'élite*, the *Lanciers de Berg*, Murat's own favourite regiment.

We early heard the popping in our front to our left, and inclined to hope that our division might soon have some nearer participation in what was passing; but it did not so happen. Like the patients of foreign pathologists under a *médecine expectants*, we were not too patiently awaiting the result, but were hoping for a further early *séance* or consideration of our present position from our French leeches.

Sir Thomas Graham commanded our wing of the army, of which our division formed the left centre and reserve, the Sixth Division and Anson's cavalry being to our left and in front; one squadron of the 14th, under Brotherton[8], and another of the 16th, under Hay and Major Cocks (considerably in advance of their supports), were on the right bank of the Azava.

The first passage of arms, which occurred that morning, arose between these troops and the enemy. The *Lanciers de Berg*, about 900 strong, advanced most rapidly. and gallantly, in order to cut off all preparatory impediments of skirmishing. The lance and sword were their weapons, they being only partially armed with carbines. The distance our advance was from its reserves, the serried phalanx of superior numbers armed with new, formidable, and hitherto unencountered weapons, induced our advance post of cavalry to retire, on the principle *de reculer pour mieux sauter.*

---

8. Now Lieutenant-General Brotherton, C.B., late Inspector of Cavalry.

They frequently however formed up and checked the too rapid advance of their foe; and then again, in compliance with orders, retired on their own brigade.

At length the enemy were encountered by our three squadrons, were charged, and promptly checked; they attempted to rally and return, when, to their no small astonishment, they received a well laid-in volley from the Light Infantry of Hulse's Brigade of the Sixth Division, composed of the light companies of the 11th, 53rd, and 61st Regiments, under Major John Mansel. These had been placed, by Sir Thomas Graham, under cover in a cork-wood on the flank of the rallying *Lanciers de Berg*, of whom sixty were rolled over by the fire of the 61st Light Company and the charge of cavalry.

Among the prisoners was Lieutenant-Colonel O'Flyn, an Irish Catholic in the French service, who, after surrendering, attempted to escape, and was killed. He evidently was of the genus Dandy, for, in stripping the body, they found that under his boots the colonel wore silk stockings. The dragoon who served as valet on the occasion offered his epaulettes to the officer of the 14th, commanding his troop, who rejected the proffered trophy, but made particular inquiries concerning Colonel O'Flyn's sudden demise, which being satisfactorily accounted for, no more was said on the subject. Another officer also was here taken; his name I forget, having made no note of it, although on arriving at Navé d'Aver he dined where I met him.

He was gay, good-looking, light-hearted, and reckless, and with so happy a disposition that he drank and sang, seeming careless, or at least unwilling to show annoyance, at being made prisoner. In one of the *mêlées* of this day a *sous-officier* of the enemy left his ranks, and singling out Brotherton, charged him. A trial of skill with the sabre ensued, each showing good knowledge of the weapon he wore.

Matters thus remained equal, till the Frenchman suddenly drew a pistol from his holster and shot Brotherton's horse through the head; it fell instantly. Brotherton quickly disengaged himself from the fallen charger, and the Frenchman was about to follow up his advantage, when another officer of the 14th, as pistols were resorted to in preference to swords, shot the Frenchman dead. The horse from which Brotherton had been dismounted by the pistol-shot was a trooper, his own having been killed or wounded the day previously; and, singular to relate, the poor wounded troop-horse recovered its consciousness, rose, trotted back, replaced himself in the rank of his troop, and fell down dead!

The above gallant rencontre and its results were witnessed by those engaged, and many are still living who remember the facts. After the charges made by the squadrons of the 14th and 16th on the *Lanciers de Berg* and the French advance guard, the latter were driven across the Azava, and our people once more re-occupied the ground of their original outposts of the morning at Carpio. On our right other matters were transacting, which I cannot better explain than by referring to a short paragraph torn Lord Wellington's despatch, under date of the 29th September, 1811, from Quadraseis. He says:—

> But the enemy's attention was principally directed during this day to the position of the Third Division on the hills between Fuente Guinaldo and Pastores. About eight in the morning they moved a column, consisting of between thirty and forty squadrons of cavalry and fourteen battalions of infantry, and twelve pieces of cannon, from Ciudad Rodrigo, in such direction that it was doubtful whether they would attempt to ascend the hills by La Encina or by the direct road of El Bodon towards Fuente Guinaldo, and I was not sure on which road they would make their attack till they actually commenced it upon the last.

From our post at Navé d'Aver our attention and our telescopes were turned to these objects. We plainly saw the advancing masses of the French approaching the heights of El Bodon, where, with a small advanced guard, Lord Wellington commanded in person. We witnessed the salute the enemy received from our guns, and marked the curling smoke rising in clouds from their brazen mouths, echoing and resounding again and again from their crested height over plain and wood and far intervening space.

At once, and suddenly, it ceased; a closer struggle and confusion ensued; then once again the destructive booming recommenced, and thus went on: now the undulating ground or elbowed point of some small promontory intercepted sound and sight together, then the kind of hog's-back formation of bill on which the operations were transacting gave us but a partial and uncertain view of what was really passing.

After about an hour's uncertainty and investment of the promontory by the enemy's numerous cavalry, at length (by force of numbers and dashing courage) we saw they had reached the ascent and gathered on its summit. Next in their turn the enemy's guns opened, and we beheld our people, surrounded by clouds of cavalry, retiring in columns and squares. After this we could no longer see distinctly what took place, but what did occur is pretty much as follows.

Marmont advanced with his columns of cavalry, directing their march to the height, on which four battalions of infantry, a brigade of Portuguese guns, and three squadrons of cavalry were posted under Lord Wellington in person. They formed part of the Third Division, consisting of the 5th and 77th British, and the 9th and 21st Portuguese Regiments, the guns under Arentschild, and the German Hussars under Victor Alten.

This height was convex towards the enemy, and covered in front and on both flanks by deep ravines.

Marmont, surrounded by his staff, advanced to the foot of this height and halted immediately beneath it, until the closing up of his infantry columns. Lord Wellington was posted immediately above this spot, and the chiefs and head-quarter staff of the two armies were not two hundred yards distant from each other. On looking over the height, every movement of the French marshal and his staff could be distinctly seen. From their proximity, as the voices ascended, the conversation carried on below could almost be overheard.

The enemy, on the contrary, could neither see what force occupied or what movements were occurring on the hill above, and had therefore no notion of what they should meet with on reaching its summit. Lord Wellington now ordered the guns to open; with good effect and unerring aim they sent their destructive messengers into Montbrun's columns of cavalry in the plain beneath; they had scarcely done so however, when a sweep of French horsemen, like a whirlwind, stormed the rocky height, charged the guns in flank, cut down the gunners at their posts, and took two cannon.

Major Ridge, commanding the 5th Regiment, a prompt and intrepid soldier, immediately brought down the bayonets of his battalion to the charge, and storming the dashing captors, drove them headlong from the rocky heights, and retook the guns. Lieutenant-Colonel Harvey[9], attached to head-quarter staff, promptly seized the occasion, and ordered the draft mules to the front; the guns were limbered up, and by the quick and gallant decision of Ridge and the ready energy of Harvey, these two guns were not only at the moment saved, but the enemy felt later the inconvenience of their being so.

While this was going on with the 5th, the 77th Regiment, under Lieutenant-Colonel Broomhead, were attacked in front by another body of the enemy's cavalry, which they repulsed by an instant advance and charge of bayonets. Again and again did the enemy storm these heights with their horsemen, but in spite of the great numerical superiority of their cavalry, they were manfully maintained by the oft-repeated and almost constant charges delivered by Victor Alten's three squadrons of the 1st German Hussars and 11th Light Dragoons. At length the enemy made a great and simultaneous effort from two opposite points at once, and, rising from the valleys beneath like some vast wave, they rushed up, and with weight and force irresistible reached the crowning plateau.

It was not until the hill had been carried by superior num-

9. In the Portuguese service at the time, now General Sir Robert Harvey, K.C.B.

bers of the enemy's cavalry, and that a division of their infantry were fast closing up for an attack, their artillery already being in action, that Lord Wellington thought proper to order the small body of troops he commanded at this post to retire on Puente Guinaldo, where he had previously thrown up some redoubts and fieldworks.

A brigade of the Fourth Division had been ordered up from Guinaldo, and the remainder of the Third Division from El Bodon, except that part of it at Pastores, which was too distant. The French cavalry, on reaching the summit, dashed on among its defenders; assailants and assailed, with the chiefs and the staff of the contending armies, seemed in the sudden *mêlée* to be thrown together in inextricable confusion.

Lord Wellington was greatly exposed at this moment, and had a narrow escape amidst the rush of French horsemen: though at first surrounded by the friendly few, he suddenly was now enveloped by the inimical many. A few yards only separated him from the charging enemy; I think it was poor Gordon[10], his *aide-de-camp*, who was said to have first pointed out the proximate danger of being captured, before Lord Wellington thought proper to turn his horse and canter off. The enemy, on reaching the height, seemed astonished at the paucity of the defenders they had so stoutly contended against, but, odd to say, profited little, as our casualties were few, and they scarcely took a single prisoner. The two weak battalions of the 5th and 77th were now thrown into one square, supported by the 21st Portuguese in solid formation of close column.

The enemy's cavalry immediately rushed forward, and obliged our cavalry to retire to the support of the Portuguese regiment., Much hard galloping ensued: the 5th and 77th were charged by the French horsemen on three faces of their square; when thus brought to bay, they halted, receiving the attack with cool, steady, and gallant bearing, repulsed it, then rose from their bristly formation, and, in phalanxed order and admirable discipline,

10. Lieutenant-Colonel the Hon. Sir Alexander Gordon, of the 3rd Guards, *aide-de-camp* to the Duke of Wellington, fell at Waterloo.

once again moved on. For six miles across an open country, in face of this superior force, did these small columns, in square, continue their march, menaced and surrounded on all sides by their enemy, and exposed to the fire of the French artillery inflicting chasms in their ranks; they quietly closed up, maintained their formation, although with diminished front, and once more moved towards the position destined for them by their great chief.

In their retreat, a shell fell into the solid column of the 21st Portuguese, and burst in its centre, destroying numbers; they opened out, left the dead or wounded, closed in again, and moved on. The Quartermaster-General, Colonel Murray[11], rode up to this regiment to give them an order, but neither the commanding nor any other officer who happened to be present, understood English sufficiently to enable him to communicate his orders to them. Captain Burgoyne[12], of the Engineers, being at hand, offered his services as a linguist, and was ordered to remain with this battalion, and directed to communicate to them the instructions to be conveyed during the remainder of these very brilliant and creditable movements. Our infantry, thus surrounded, conducted themselves in as cool and orderly a manner as at a field-day; those present declared they never saw a more beautiful sight. Such is the worth of steady discipline!

The French cavalry were now galloping in forward movement all over the field, out-flanking our cavalry and infantry, pressing on our rear, and in all parts became inconveniently disturbing and obtrusive. To sportsmen, and the many home-bred seekers of action and excitement, I may here relate an episode of adventure, midst more serious matters of the kind, which occurred that morning.

Lord Charles Manners, extra *aide-de-camp* to Lord Wellington, in a most sportsman-like manner escaped from being made prisoner. By hard work his horse had been knocked up, and he rode to the rear, where he had posted his fresh one, to get a remount;

---

11. Afterwards the Right Hon. Lieutenant-General Sir George Murray, G.C.B., M.P.
12. Now Lieutenant-General Sir John Burgoyne, G.C.B., Inspector of Fortifications.

on returning, he met an officer of artillery, who informed him where he would find Lord Wellington (this was on the hill immediately above them, over which he was retreating with our troops); the artillery officer, however, advised him by no means to go in a direct line, as he must, in such case, throw himself and his newly-remounted charger right into the range of fire of three French howitzers which had just opened upon our retiring columns.

On this, Lord Charles took a slanting direction, and turned the hill, instead of going directly up it, but on rounding a small declivity he came plump upon two squadrons of French Chasseurs *à Cheval*; he instantly drew up his horse (a capital hunter) from a canter to a walk, and at that pace quietly proceeded on to reconnoitre. On arriving within some thirty yards of the enemy, however, the French General, Déjean, commanding these troops, accompanied by four orderlies, had stationed himself at their head in advance, and called out, "*Que cherchez-vous, Monsieur?*"

The gallant *aide-de-camp* replied, "Milord Wellington."

The general immediately made a signal with his sword, pointing out Lord Charles to his orderlies, who galloped forward to take him, but he turned his horse; and, knowing the country, led them across a difficult part and towards a nasty wide yawning water-course, still keeping the direction in which he believed Lord Wellington to be. The pursuing four pressed on, and when within hopeful distance of catching the pursued, to their astonishment they saw his horse flying in the air over the vast chasm, which, becoming to them an impassable barrier, brought them up to a standstill.

Alava, on the hill above, seeing the pursuit, and what was passing beneath, not knowing the confidence placed in his horse by Lord Charles, sent down some Spanish guerrillas, who soon induced the baffled pursuers to return hastily under cover of their numerous friends; whilst Lord Charles, in a quiet canter, continued his course and joined Lord Wellington.

Some of the rest of the Third Division had now joined, and

also forming squares, the whole continued to retire. Soon after they were met by the Fourth Division advancing to their support: under the fire of the enemy's artillery, and environed by their cavalry, they still continued their retreat to the ground near Puente Guinaldo.

Here Lord Wellington had already caused two redoubts and some fieldworks to be thrown up: orders had been sent to the Light Division to retire from Vadillo, with which that gallant but unmanageable Chief of Division, Craufurd, did not think proper to comply. With or without reason, he really liked fighting, and never threw away a chance of bringing a "scrimmage" about; he always held to his own ideas, and loved to see his name in the Gazette.

With many sterling and soldierlike qualities, he was the sublime of the refractory and provokingly useful. The consequence of all this delay created much inconvenience and no small danger to Lord Wellington, who had taken up the position at Guinaldo, and awaited Craufurd's joining him. The deployment of Marmont's forces towards this point became threatening; but, at all events, Lord Wellington would not and could not move further to the rear until assured of the safety of the Light Division. Separated, and at a distance, Craufurd's procrastination to obey orders very nearly occasioned him to be cut off from the rest of our army; and he had to make a considerable detour and a night-march to retrieve himself, and regain his communication with Lord Wellington.

Here again was exemplified the necessity of prompt obedience to the chief in command, whose designs and reasons the commanders of separate corps may not at the moment be able to comprehend. In the meantime Lord Wellington, having regained his entrenchments about four o'clock p.m., the enemy, whose activity in favouring the retreating columns with round shot and shell had been excessive, halted and ceased firing. While this was going on upon our right, the advance of the left wing of the army, under Graham, was ordered to fall back on our division at Navé d'Aver, leaving cavalry outposts on the Azava, and thus we passed the night.

On the 26th, in the morning, Lord Wellington still held his post at Guinaldo with only the Third and Fourth Divisions, some cavalry, and guns; in all about 14,000 men. No news of the Light Division had as yet reached Lord Wellington; he therefore held his ground, deploying his troops to make them look more numerous than they were,—in short, making as imposing an appearance to his enemy as he could. The concentrated and overwhelming numbers of the enemy had been brought to bear on this one single point of the extended divisions of our army. Sixty thousand Frenchmen, with great superiority of cavalry and 100 guns, stood immediately before, and their sentries and *vedettes* in actual and immediate contact with those of the two divisions commanded by Lord Wellington in person.

This certainly was a most anxious and critical moment: all eyes were turned to the front, in momentary expectation of a crushing attempt being made on our small force, when Lord Wellington, seemingly tired of waiting, and feeling drowsy, told one of his *aides-de-camp* to call him if anything was the matter, wrapped himself in his cloak, lay down in the broiling sun, and slept very composedly and soundly for more than two hours[13]. For some unknown reason, Marmont made no attack this day; he did not seem to know the positions of our different divisions, was deceived by the appearances displayed by our chief, and was otherwise mystified.

Of the operations of the 27th, Lord Wellington writes as follows:—

It had been the enemy's intention to turn the left of the position of Guinaldo, by moving a column into the valley of the Upper Azava, and thence ascending the height in the rear of the position by Castillejos; and from this

---

13. The greatest general of antiquity possessed a similar power of sleeping when he would, or rather when he could. *Livy* (21. 4) *records of Hannibal,* "*Vigiliarum somnique nee die, nee nocte discriminata tempore. Id quod gerendis rebus superesset quieti datum: eaque neque molli stratu, neque silentio arcessita. Multi sæpe, militari sagulo opertum, humi jacentem inter custodias stationesque militum, conspexerunt.*"

column they detached a division of infantry and fourteen regiments of cavalry to follow our retreat by Albergueria, and another body of the same strength followed us by Forcalhos. The former attacked the piquets of the cavalry at Aldea da Ponte, and drove them in; and they pushed on nearly as far as Alfyates. I then made General Pakenham attack them with his brigade of the Fourth Division, supported by Lieutenant-General the Hon. L. Cole and the Fourth Division, and by Sir S. Cotton's[14] cavalry; and the enemy were driven through Aldea da Ponte, back upon Albergueria, and the piquets of the cavalry resumed their station.

But the enemy having been reinforced by the troops which marched from Forcalhos, again advanced about sunset, and drove in the piquets of the cavalry from Aldea da Ponte, and took possession of the village. Lieutenant-General Cole again attacked them, with a part of General Pakenham's brigade, and drove them through the village; but night having come on, and as General Pakenham was not certain what was passing on his flanks, or of the numbers of the enemy, and he knew that the army were to fall back still farther, he evacuated the village, which the enemy occupied, and held during the night.

There had been this day some very heavy skirmishing at Aldea da Ponte; and in this sharp affair, among others, Captain Prevost, son of Sir George, and *aide-de-camp* to Sir Lowry Cole, was killed. On this night, the 27th, I was on piquet in front of Navé d'Aver, when, about ten o' clock, an order came to withdraw the outposts. Our division made a night march of six hours, and halted at Bismuda, in rear of Villa Major.

On the 26th the army were all concentrated in a very strong position on the heights behind Soito, having the Sierra de Mesas on their right and Rendo on the Coa on our left A loop of the river covered both flanks; and, in addition, rough, rocky, and

---

14. Now Lord Combermere.

woody ground impeded the advance of the enemy in front. The most singular circumstance was, that the enemy commenced their retreat at the very same time that we did, and we were each moving away from one another!

It is not my intention to enter into the merits of the tactics displayed on this occasion, for much superlatively fine military criticism has been bestowed upon these movements. One strategic censor thinks that the position on which Lord Wellington meant to retire, and perhaps fight, with a river in his rear, was objectionable; another, that his contempt for his enemy led him into a hazardous imprudence; and a third, that if Marmont had done this, and if he had done that, neither of which he did do, why, something else would have probably resulted.

These suggestions may or may not be sound: the movements may not have been upon military principles strictly correct; but the argument of what might have happened, but which did not happen, is like entering into that complicated point, that if your aunt was not your aunt, she might have been your uncle. The fact was, that Lord Wellington on this occasion placed himself *hors de règle,* and acquired the knowledge he wished to obtain, while the enemy had no knowledge of him; his own quickness, and the excellence of his troops, rendered such a liberty at least-warrantable.

All movements depended upon supply. He knew that the enemy wanted means to support an army together for any length of time. Ignorant as Marmont was of the precise whereabouts of Lord Wellington's divisions, he perfectly well knew that if a successful action had been fought, it would scarcely have led him into Portugal; where there was as little to be found to sustain life, as poor James Macdonald of the Guards discovered when he opened an economical general's cupboard, and found two lean mice contemplating, with tears in their eyes, a hard crust of bread!

Lord Wellington was master of his circumstances, was aware of his enemy's ignorance, knew no serious attempt could at that moment be made on Portugal by Marmont; he therefore put on a bold front, made an imposing appearance, and gained his object without any great loss. I find the following paragraph in an old letter of mine, written just before these movements, and dated from Navé d'Aver, the 24th of September, 1811, addressed to a general officer in England:—

The enemy are advancing with a convoy for Ciudad Rodrigo. Report also says, that they are in movement in the Alemtejo; but I will make two bets. One is, that whatever force the French can bring (and Marmont is reported to have 60,000 men in our front), they will not attempt to enter Portugal; and the next is, that if they try, we shall not fight till we reach a position on the Coa. God knows what will be the result; I do not mean the result in case of fighting, for that we are all confident about, but the result of their advance. By the bye, it is said that the Duke of Leinster, Lords Delaware and Clare, and Henry Fitzgerald[15] have landed at Lisbon, and are all on their way up to see the army. A very nice time they have chosen for their trip! No baggage, much movement, short commons, and no respect of personages. *Adieu!* I am called away.

The first part of this letter was perfectly verified by what I have related in the foregoing pages.

---

15. Afterwards Lord De Ros.

# CHAPTER 7

# A Winter March

During this campaign we had many amateurs, or T.G.s as they would be called in modern phraseology, whose curiosity far exceeded their cognizance of military position; one of these found himself suddenly one fine morning in the midst of a French instead of an English out-piquet. Although arriving early, and quite unexpectedly, he was politely requested to remain and make a sojourn with them; he pleaded his non-combative qualities, protested "*qu'il n'était pas du tout, du tout militaire*," laid great stress upon his love of the peaceful, the beautiful, the picturesque; that he was a mere wanderer to see the country and the war, and assured the French officer he was "*purement un amateur.*"

He who had charge of the Gallic outpost, however, was incredulous and uninfluenced by such sophistry, and could not understand such a fine-drawn distinction in so doubtful a predicament; besides, our unlucky countryman had adopted a military costume,—a blue coat, cocked hat, and sword,—which rendered his belligerent appearance more complete, and his peaceable pretensions less credible. Although later in life (*tempora mutantur!*) he might have declared himself one of "Bright and Cobden's own," at the time all his protestations were in vain. To the head-quarters of the enemy's army he was sent a prisoner.

Not long previous to this, a French lieutenant-colonel had been taken by some of our people. When our unfortunate traveller reached his destination, a flag of truce was sent to Lord Wellington from the French marshal, saying that they had taken a prisoner, calling himself an amateur; that the marshal did not clearly comprehend what that name implied, as they had none such in their army; but if Lord Wellington would exchange him for the lieutenant-colonel lately taken from them, the marshal would return the amateur. Lord Wellington is stated to have answered, that he was "much obliged to the French commander for the proposition, but he begged he would keep him."

I do remember however an amateur whose thorough English feeling led him, at Waterloo, into the thick of the fight; and whose activity, usefulness, and gallantry were conspicuous throughout the whole of that eventful day. In a plain blue coat, and round hat, he had ridden that morning from Brussels, joined the Duke on the field, and attached himself to him.

As the staff of the great hero began to fall around him, and casualties occurred to man and horse, he supplied their place, and conveyed orders for the Duke to different parts of the field. This circumstance was well known at the time to all, and ought to be perpetuated, for none more honourably or honestly earned distinction that day than the present Earl Bathurst, then Lord Apsley. May other amateurs, in future wars, emulate so chivalrous and patriotic an example!

But to return from this digression. After the convoy and the fresh garrison had been thrown into Ciudad Rodrigo, Marmont had no object, and Lord Wellington quite as little temptation, to fight. If the French marshal had accomplished his purpose, the English general had equally obtained his end, having acquired, by personal observation, a knowledge of the amount of force the enemy could bring into the field, when the moment should arrive for his contemplated attack on Ciudad Rodrigo.

The weather was now cold and rainy; the 28th would have been a beautiful day for ducks and hackney-coachmen; had either been in the neighbourhood, we certainly should have roasted, beyond a joke, the former interesting absentees, and availed ourselves of the services of the latter in consideration of the want of umbrellas in the army!

We moved to Rendo; on the 29th crossed the Coa to Gata,

and on the 30th reached Val des Ayres,—a pretty village situated between Celorico and Guarda, hanging on the slope, and at the foot of a ridge or spur thrown out from the Serra d'Estrella towards the Val de Mondego. This, as far as the picturesque went, was certainly a most beautiful country. The French having retired to Salamanca, Banos, and Plasencia, our outposts were left to watch Ciudad Rodrigo, and Lord Wellington established his head-quarters at Frenada.

These, our retiring movements from the frontier of Portugal, were intended to lull Marshal Marmont into security, and the belief of our peaceable intentions for the rest of the winter; we therefore arrived at our pretty village in the Val de Mondego under the false pretext of making it our winter quarters, as the autumnal rains had set in. In the absence of more military or exciting exploits, we were disposed to recognize the truthful philosophy of two lines we found written on an old door in an empty house, by some French *gaillard*:

*Heureux, heureux, celui qui, bien loin de la guerre,*
*Goûte d'un petit plat et boit dans un grand verre!*

Our only difficulty was, as an American would say, "to realize to ourselves" so pleasant a practice. The army was three months in arrear of pay; bills on England were difficult to cash, and at a villainous exchange of six shillings for the dollar, of which the current value was five; comestibles were difficult to procure; and luxuries, such as tea, sugar, brandy, etc., to be found only on occasions of the few-and-far-between visits of sutlers who followed the army.

One fellow of this calling, an Italian, enjoying the murderous name of Sanguinetti, was the most constant of his kind, and the most extortionate in his constancy; his visits, in their long intervals of uncertainty, bespoke more of the Jew than the angel; that is, in ministering to our wants he had a lively sense of his own interests, his motto evidently being—

*Con arte e con inganno*
*Si vive mezzo l'anno,*

*Con inganno e con arte*
*Si vive l'altra parte.*

He was however one of those necessary evils on which fellows who rough it, and have no choice, will fall back occasionally. Another battalion of our brigade was quartered at no great distance, at the village of Lagiosa; our interchange of visits and good fellowship was frequent, but our means of hospitality were few; however, those fellows of our division, the Guards, were accused of "roughing it on a beefsteak and a bottle of port," which, no doubt, they always did, like the rest of the army, when they could get it, but never otherwise; *Apropos* to "the gentlemen's sons," as they were called, I may here narrate an anecdote in allusion to them, although it did not occur till many years after in England.

At a supper at Hatfield House, in Hertfordshire, Sir John S——, Bart., and Colonel H. B——, afterwards Lord D——, entered into an animated discussion on the respective merits of the Guards and the line; they became warm in defence of their individual opinions, and at last appealed to the Duke of Wellington, who was present. "Oh!" he said, "I am all for the Guards—all for the Guards."
One of the disputants rejoined, "I told you so; those fellows in silk stockings and shoes have more blood about them, and blood will tell."
"Ah!" said the Duke, "I did not mean that; I meant the non-commissioned officers."

The Duke certainly gave strong proof of his estimation of the merits and good conduct of the non-commissioned officers of the Guards; for during the period I happened to serve with the First Division of the army, to which the Second Brigade of Guards belonged, he recommended for commissions, as adjutants, quarter-masters, and subalterns in different regiments, no less than fourteen non-commissioned officers of that brigade. The Duke, on this occasion, seeing the disputants were heated, probably-meant to turn the warm discussion into pleasantry, and availed himself of the merits of the non-commissioned officers for that purpose; for no man's estimation of the Guards as an entire corps was higher than that of the Duke of Wellington himself.

However possible it may be to meet with a heaven-born Minister of State (although I confess I really never saw one), he knew right well that in a less exalted situation there were no such things as heaven-born non-commissioned officers: somebody must have created them after their birth.

If the commanding officers, adjutants, captains, and subalterns did not maintain the discipline, and keep up the system which formed the non-commissioned officers, who else did? The estimation in which the Duke seemed to hold this small portion of his army may be gathered from a reference to his general orders, his despatches, and the way in which he always spoke of them as a body.

No one could accuse the Duke of being prone to compliment; downright and truthful expression was his forte; and as he seemed to think the first might deteriorate from the last, he made no use of it. He was much more given to saying what he thought of things and persons, than some people found it convenient to hear; and whenever a man desired to deeply impress his own merit upon the Duke, he was pretty sure to have, in return, in terse and concise words, the Duke's estimation of him.

From this it may be collected that, in like manner, when he did speak favourably, it might be relied upon as equally proceeding from the sound conviction of his own mind, and that he considered the interest of truth better served by facts than by fables. Baron Müffling narrates one of these short expressions of his confidence and reliance, which I will venture to copy here.

He states this to have happened between the Duke and himself on the field of Waterloo, in the morning, immediately after the action had commenced, and says that he "spoke with the Duke after the battle had begun, about the strength and weakness of his line of battle;" and goes on to state, "not fearing for his centre and left wing, I considered his right wing the weakest point, and Hougoumont, in particular, I deemed untenable in a serious assault by the enemy.

This the Duke disputed, as he had. put the old *château* in a state of defence, and caused the long garden-wall towards the field of battle to be crenellated; and he added, 'I have thrown *Macdonell*[1] into it,' an officer on whom he placed especial reliance."

Lieutenant-Colonel Macdonell, of the Coldstream, commanded the light infantry companies of the Second Brigade of Guards in Hougoumont: the Duke's expression therefore conveys a reliance not only on the officer in command, but on the troops he commanded.

None on that day of trial, in conduct, endurance, or discipline, were more severely tested than those who perseveringly held this post against repeated attacks by overwhelming numbers.

Credit therefore must be accorded as due through each grade, from rank-and-file to rank of commander, to those who so well fulfilled the duty expected of them and the confidence placed in them by their great commander;[2] those not in the *château* equally responded to his call, and gained his approbation, as all good troops of every corps and every arm did on that day.

In a paragraph from his *Waterloo despatch* he says:

"It gives me the greatest satisfaction to assure your lordship" (the Secretary for War and Colonies, then Lord Bathurst), "that the army never upon any occasion conducted itself better. The division of Guards under Lieutenant-General Cooke[3], who is severely wounded, Major General Mait-

---

1. Lieutenant-General Sir James Macdonell, K.C.B., K.C.H., Colonel of the 71st Regiment.
2. This was afforded at the close of the action by the Duke himself. Baron Müffling goes on to narrate:—
"I met the Duke in the neighbourhood of La Have Sainte, holding a telescope in his right hand; he called out to me from a distance, 'Well! you see Macdonell has held Hougoumont.' This was an expression of pleasure that his brave comrade had answered his expectations."
3. Afterwards Sir George Cooke, K.C.B.; lost an arm at Waterloo.

land[4], and Major General Byng[5], set an example which was followed by all[6]."

As to controversies concerning the merits of individual corps in relation to each other, I confess I condemn them. Where all act well and perform their duty, the only cause of emulative dispute should be how to serve their country best by licking her enemies the most. This is the goal to be reached; the rest is all twaddle.

But *retournons à nos moutons* at Val des Ayres. The autumnal rains set in, and the weather was very bad. There was at this time a good deal of sickness in the ranks of our army; for example, out of my own company alone, in strength sixty-six rank-and-file and four officers, thirty of the former were sick absent and two sick present, and of the four latter I was the only one doing duty, one being wounded and a prisoner, and two sick at Coimbra. In our battalion there were at this time, of officers, ten sick absent, four sick present, one prisoner, one invalided, and two just dead; and this in proportion was pretty much the same in other corps.

I here had a touch of the ague, but a light heart and Lamego wine soon made this enemy retire. At this time too I was much pressed to try and obtain leave to go home on some important family matters; but that I also successfully resisted, although the temptation certainly was great, to see once more friends and home; however, I stuck to my colours and the service, feeling, from the dearth of officers, that I could not be conveniently

---

4. General Sir Peregrine Maitland, G.C.B., Colonel of the 17th Regiment
5. Now General the Earl of Strafford, G.C.B. etc. etc., Colonel of the Coldstream Regiment of Guards.
6. The expression attributed to the Duke, "Up Guards, and at them again!" I have good reason for knowing was never made use of by him. He was not even with the Brigade of Guards in question at the time they rose from their recumbent position to attack the French column in their front, and therefore could not well have thus addressed them. I never heard this story till long after, on my return to England, when it was related by a lady at a dinner-table; probably it was the invention of some goodly Botherby. I remember denying my belief in it at the time, and my view has since been sufficiently confirmed. Besides, the words bear no internal evidence of the style either of thought or expression of him to whom they were attributed.

spared. I did not choose to apply for leave of absence; and being fairly embarked in my profession, it would have annoyed me to have been absent while active and brilliant operations were going on, and we pretty well knew that our pretended winter-quarters were all a blind. I therefore remained, in failure of others, in command of my company.

I had some troublesome although amusing characters to control. Two of them I especially remember: one an Irishman, M'Culloch, whose cap had been carried off by a shell at Fuentes d'Oñor; the other a Scotchman, by name Campbell. These two fellows were comrades, although quite opposite characters; each retained the unmistakeable type of his nation; the opposite quality of disposition was soothed by the mutual love of ebriosity. This made the intimacy more piquant.

Pat was all *blatheremskite*, as they called it in his fatherland, with some wit, great good humour, and the smallest possible powers of calculation. Campbell was a clever, long-headed, canny Scot, and well educated,—so much so as to have in his knapsack a small well-thumbed edition of Horace. This seemed to him in his soberer hours a great resource; from it he would quote to his comrades most unintelligible conversation, which, in his hard, dry manner, was most amusingly conveyed.

Campbell, through his powers of arithmetic, became the honoured *homme d'affaires* of his friend M'Culloch; and when pay-day arrived, Campbell received the money from the pay-sergeant, and explained the particulars to his friend. The first impulse with both on receiving money was, immediately to get drunk; and, do what one could, by remonstrance or punishment, this was not to be prevented.

When drunk, they were most joyously loving friends; but as soon as drunkenness ceased to be drunk, Campbell could never make M'Culloch understand the "Spee-cialities" of the account between them, when on the wrong side of his ledger. They were regularly brought up to me to see justice done; I generally first accomplished this by punishing them both for inebriety, but their wrangling often put to the test all my powers of gravity.

The Irishman's real or pretended want of comprehension, larded with the most ridiculous expressions and witty remarks,— the Scotchman's grave face, cool logic, and authentic arithmetic, pushed with keenness to demonstration,—was a never-failing scene served up monthly to my notice.

In those days the very in-exclusive mode of recruiting the army brought us acquainted with many ineligible characters; the necessities of the war being great, scruples against enlistment were few,—all were fish that came to the net, and all were indiscriminately taken. Many fine, gallant, good fellows enlisted from right and proper motived, and did well; but still, as casualties by sickness and the sword prevented the supply from keeping pace with the demand, at last anything was taken: even manumitted gaol-birds were admitted as "food for powder."

This portion of the British army carried along with it its inconveniences, both in bad example and the necessity of its repression. The maintenance of discipline on service is a very different affair from managing the system of regularity accomplished at home or in colonial garrisons. It is to the previous tiresome attention to trifles that is to be attributed the acquired habit of punctuality, order, and obedience. The persevering, unvarying system instils into the mind of the soldier at last, not merely the physical, but the moral obligation in the performance of a requisite duty. From such training it is that good soldiers are afterwards made: with the Englishman this takes time, and requires opportunities which do not occur on service; for then different and far greater difficulties arise in maintaining even the groundwork that had been established.

Much depends not only on individual character, but on the depth with which that character has been imbued (not to say inoculated) with the proper virus. In a campaign an immediate change ensues, a strain upon all former pipe-clay ordinances occurs,—more discretionary power being left at the disposition of the soldier in taking care of himself, instead of being taken care of; he is more his own master; necessity then becomes the mother of contrivance; they have a thousand things to learn for themselves which cannot be taught in barracks and garrisons, and are most essential acquirements to enable men to meet the hardships they encounter.

To obtain the knowledge, under all circumstances, to shift for themselves; to make the most out of a little; to economize rest and food when opportunity affords them; to show invention and adaptation of means to ends, and a conservation and economy of their physical powers; to maintain a healthy body, sound feet, and a strong stomach, reserving, according to their means, always something to put into it; in short, to keep themselves, under difficult circumstances, in good bodily condition;—all this has to be learned by the young soldier and officer.

On this point the Duke of Wellington was reported to have said, "that he would rather have one man who had served two campaigns, than two men who had not served one."

While on this subject I may remark, that without food or drink there is no one of Heaven's creation who feels so small as an Englishman; whether it proceeds from want of habit of abstinence, or construction of stomach, the fact was evident. In other nations the early habit of vegetable diet in preference to animal food, the temperament of blood, or the effect of climate, seems to render them better able to support this kind of privation. To make an Englishman march up to his mark, or fight up to his habits, you must feed him: if you do not, he will plunder, for go without it he will not[7]. I have seen Spaniards, Portuguese, French, and even Germans, support this species of hardship better than the English soldier; he and his horse stand training in

---

7. As instance of which, I will here give the Duke's opinion, on the authority of Baron Müffling, who says, that after Waterloo, "on the march to Paris, the Prussian army made longer marches than the English; and when in the morning I made my daily communications to the Duke, I took the liberty of respectfully calling his attention to this, and suggesting that it would be better if he kept the same pace as his ally. He was silent at first, but on my urging him again to move more rapidly, he said to me, 'Do not press me on this point, for I tell you it won't do. If you were better acquainted with the English army, its composition and habits, you would say the same. I cannot separate from my tents and my supplies. My troops must be well kept and well supplied in camp, if order and discipline are to be maintained. It is better that I should arrive two days later in Paris, than that discipline should be relaxed.'"

this way worse than any others.

Another material consideration on service is the men's shoes. After the battle of Salamanca a circumstance occurred to the First Division of the army in relation to this. With no immediate means at hand to supply them with others, they had fairly marched their shoes off; they adopted the system of the Spanish muleteers, and resorted to the raw hides of the fresh-killed bullocks, which had been slaughtered for their food. They placed their foot on the warm hide, and cut out a sufficiency to cover this most vulnerable part of a soldier's person, and making a sandal of it marched on with ease and glee.

Afterwards the difficulty was, when French shoes were taken at the surrender of the Retiro at Madrid, to induce the men to quit the easy, well-fitting, and pliant sandal, for the hard and cumbrous leather shoe. Wisely and advantageously to palliate and correct the ills that troops in war are heir to, is no easy undertaking.

The difficulties are not to be appreciated until officers and men are fairly embarked in the reality of a Continental campaign; endurance of severe privation at one moment, and exposure to temptation at another, are great disturbers of health and discipline.

Morally and physically to bear and forbear is the lesson to be learned,—this is the real *morale en action:* to tame down the turbulent, and cultivate a good feeling in the well disposed, are the duties of the officer, amidst want, fatigue, and demoralizing influences. He should have tact and discrimination, and a knowledge of the characters of those under him. Punishments on service will vary as much as those who may deserve them; and the manner of putting in force what crime may well merit and example exact, is often difficult and sometimes detrimental, paradoxical as the case may appear.

The main point, however, is to keep up as kindly and good a feeling between all grades as is possible; and when I talk of punishment, I will not inflict one on my reader by helping him to so somniferous a subject as a treatise on discipline, but shall leave that to those whose duty it may be. All I have to observe in this case is, the immense improvement, since the time of which I write, which has been made in the discipline and moral educational instruction of our army.

*October 22nd.*—We heard at this time of a stealthy, clever operation carried out by our friend Don Julian Sanchez, of guerrilla fame, who closely watched the French garrison of Ciudad Rodrigo; In the night the enemy were accustomed to send forth from the town their live-stock to feed on the glacis, their custom being to withdraw them within the town again as daylight broke; Julian Sanchez having obtained information of this, laid wait with his horsemen, pounced one dark rainy night upon the supping quadrupeds, killed those in charge of them, and drove off nearly two hundred bullocks from under the very guns of the fortress.

This loss being made evident to the Governor next morning, he came out himself, with an escort, to reconnoitre; and, when at no great distance beyond the range of his own artillery, they suddenly received an unexpected and equally *impromptu* visit from the same guerrilla chief, who, having killed and wounded some in the onslaught, took all the rest prisoners, including General Renaud and his two *aides-de-camp*; but afterwards the two last contrived to make their escape. The Light, Third, and Fourth Divisions were at this time between the Coa and the Agueda, distantly watching the garrison of Rodrigo. The First, Fifth, Sixth, and Seventh, together with the greater part of our artillery, were placed, for the sake of provisions, in an extended order from the frontier to as far back as the Val de Mondego.

The rainy season set in with all its wonted vigour: tremendous storms of thunder and' wind drove the rain against the barren mountains by which we were surrounded; these last disgorged what they received in foaming watercourses, descending in jumping torrents past dwellings beneath, and rendering both rivers and roads impassable. Few of the cottages we were destined to inhabit could be considered in that state of repair that English architects would considerately pronounce wind, water, or weather proof.

However, to be under cover at all in such a season was a luxury which did not last very long. On the 1st November we received orders to march next morning to Açores, and from thence to proceed to bivouac near Gata. We commenced our march, and had nearly reached Lagiosa, when we were happily countermanded, and very thankfully returned to Graciosa and Val des Ayres.

From its want of novelty the prospect of bivouacking in a mist, with spongy ground for a bed, could always be dispensed with by us without regret. Such anticipations remind me of a learned acquaintance of mine, of antiquarian propensities, who, in perfect seriousness, on visiting Rome, declared he did not think that the interior of the Pantheon looked comfortable! What my worthy friend meant to predicate by this is not easy to determine—probably that he found in his temporary visits small "indoor relief," to use a union-house phrase; while, on the other hand, in bad weather we had a constant lively sense of the inconveniences of "the outdoor" system.

Soon after our return to our lately left quarter, we heard of General Hill's[8] successful surprise in the south of General Girard's force at Arroyo Molinos. These movements were well planned and equally well executed. A small movable column, under Girard, had been foraging between the Tagus and the Guadiana, in the neighbourhood of Caceres, and preventing our allies, the Spaniards, under Morillo, from supporting his troops from that quarter.

Lord Wellington ordered Hill to drive the enemy away, who advanced, on the 26th of October, to Malpertida de Caceres for that purpose. The enemy withdrew to Arroyo Molinos, leaving a rear-guard at Albala. Hill saw his advantage, and promptly seized it, by a forced night march on a shorter parallel road, and reached, without their knowledge, Alcuesca, only a league distant from the enemy[9]. The village of Arroyo was situated in

8. Afterwards Lord Hill, Commander-in-Chief of the Army.
9. See *Napier*.

a plain, and behind it a *sierra*, or ridge of rocks, rose in the form of a crescent.

During the night, though the weather was dreadful, no fires were permitted in the Allied camp, and at two o'clock in the morning of the 28th, the troops moved to a low ridge, only half a mile distant from Arroyo. Behind this they formed into three columns, the infantry on the flanks, the cavalry in the centre; and before daylight, on a misty, stormy October morning, which favoured their approach, the left wing moved direct upon the enemy, while the other infantry column and cavalry, with the guns, directed their march to the right, and intercepted the enemy's retreat by flanking it, and reached the other side, with the view of entirely cutting off their escape.

One brigade of Girard's had marched early in the morning, and were out of harm's way, but the rest, Dambrouski's infantry and Briche's cavalry, were found in happy ignorance of danger, comfortably preparing for their march, their horses of the rear-guard unbridled and tied to olive-trees, the infantry only gathering to form outside on the Medellin road, and Girard himself in his quarters waiting to mount his horse, when Howard's Brigade, the 50th, 71st, and 92nd entered pell-mell amongst them, the last two regiments charging down the street, and the Highland pibrochs singing forth the old Jacobite air of "Johnny Cope, are ye rising yet?"

The enemy,—that is, those who could escape,—after some hard fighting and struggling, were driven to the end of the village, the 50th securing those who had been captured. The remainder of the French formed in squares outside, and covered the main body of their horsemen on the left, Cadogan, with the 71st, lined the garden-walls, and opened a galling fire on the nearest square; the 92nd cleared the village, and formed upon the enemy's right; the Spanish cavalry skirted the houses, to endeavour to intercept their line of retreat.

The guns opened on the French squares; our 13th Dragoons captured their artillery; the 9th Dragoons and 2nd German Hussars charged their cavalry, and entirely dispersed it with great loss; Girard was wounded, but still kept his infantry together, and continued his retreat by the Truxillo road; his men were falling by fifties, and his situation was desperate, but on further retiring he found the road closed by the right column of the Allies, while Howard's Brigade were pressing and coming up fast on his front.

Nothing being left for it, the enemy now, sooner than surrender, broke, and throwing away their arms and knapsacks, endeavoured to escape singly by scaling the almost inaccessible rocks of the sierra, which over-topped the village and the roads. They were pursued even in this attempt, by the 28th and 34th, led by General Howard, who followed them step by step up the rocks, and many prisoners were made. Girard, wounded, and Dambrouski and Briche escaped with about 600 out of 3000 men, and after wandering in the Guadalupe mountains, crossed the Guadiana at Orrelano, and joined Drouet. The spoil was, all the French artillery, baggage, and commissariat, together with two generals taken (Brun and Prince d'Arenberg), thirty other officers, and 1300 prisoners. A private of the 92nd took Prince d'Arenberg.

The loss of the Allies was not more than seventy killed and wounded; but Strenowitz of the German Hussars, to whom I have before alluded as having distinguished himself, being on this occasion too forward in the pursuit, was made prisoner. On the application however of General Hill to General Drouet, the latter kindly released him. Lord Hill, speaking of the troops under him in his despatch to Lord Wellington, says:—

No praise of mine can do justice to their admirable conduct; the patience and goodwill shown by all ranks during forced marches in the worst of weather, their strict attention to the orders they received, the precision with which they moved to the attack, and their obedience to command during the action; in short, the manner in which everyone has performed his duty from the first commencement of the operations, merits my warmest thanks, and will not, I am sure, be passed unobserved by your Lordship.

On the 24th of November we suddenly received an order to move; we were to leave our baggage behind at Val des Ayres, and to march directly in advance to the frontier. It was a hard frost, and the weather was severely cold; we left Graciosa about midday, to climb one of those bleak offshoot ranges of the Serra d'Estrella, the top of which last is, in summer and winter, covered with snow. In our ascent, we faced the iced wind rushing down from the mountain's hoary head, which was sufficient to cool the hottest temper, or chill the warmest heart: keen and piercing were the effects to those exposed to it.

Over this wild, barren country, we this day marched six long Portuguese *leagues*, equivalent to twenty-four English miles, and did not reach till midnight the miserable village of Regiosa, where we halted.

Being very unwell, and only just recovered from an inflammation of the chest, followed by ague and fever, I remember this day's march right well: great weakness and raging headache were my disagreeable companions in this day's pedestrianism. It was too cold to mount my horse, and I led him. On our arrival we had two companies and three officers of our battalion put under cover at this poor place: it could hold no more, and scarcely even these. The rest were dispersed about in different small villages, so as to put our men under roofs,—a desirable object, as far as health went, at this season, in these cold and mountainous regions. In thus dispersing the troops, by some blundering our two companies found themselves deserted by the commissary, and were left without rations.

Those men who had the *savoir-faire* about them, and had economized their prior stock of biscuit, now conveniently discovered it, perhaps at the bottom of their haversacks; but those who had not, were left for six-and-thirty hours without food, or any means of procuring it. Luckily I discovered in my portable larder (a fishing basket attached to my horse's saddle) one biscuit and a small piece of cheese, which was divided amongst three of us; then, thanking our stars that we were on the right side of the door of a house, we made in our smoky hovel the best fire we could, stretched ourselves on the ground in our cloaks before it, and slept till daylight roused us once more to renew our march.

We moved three leagues to Aldea de Dona, and next day to Navé d'Aver. The occasion of our thus closing up to the frontier, was the assembly, in the neighbourhood of Tamames, of some 14,000 of the enemy, to convey fresh cattle and a commander into Ciudad Rodrigo, in lieu of those lately filched from that fortress by Julian Sanchez. Lord Wellington fully meant to cross the Azava and the Agueda, to attack them with his whole force, in their charitable attempt to succour their friends, for which purpose all our divisions had been moved in concentration to between the Coa and Agueda; but, unluckily, the weather had been so bad, and the rain so abundant, that it rendered the fords of the Azava and Agueda impassable. Taking advantage of this, General Thiebault seized the occasion, introduced the convoy and the new Governor General Barrie, and precipitately retired, before we could get at him across these waters.

Having previously, in winter, been in the south of Portugal, or the neighbourhood of Lisbon, we were unaccustomed to sharp cold; and on reaching the high plateau of open country, on which Navé de Aver stands, we felt it more severely. The rivers remained flooded, but the frost was still as hard as in a more northern latitude; the hovels of Navé d'Aver formed but a polite excuse for a covering.

We sat, when indoors (for in-windows we could not call it, there being none beyond broken shutters), wrapped in our cloaks, on the family household chests of the poor inhabitants, round a *brazarico,* or pan of hot ashes, to warm the extremities of man; a joke or a cigar in our mouth, to console the stomach or brush up the intellect; our drink, when we could get it, some kind of wine or alcohol, to fill the internal portion of human nature's commissariat *depôt.*

These, together with a sincere good wish for a better abode, a battle, or anything, in short, that would circulate the blood or interest the mind, formed our *desiderata;* though we bore our hardships with the true spirit of well-tried, red-coated philosophers.

As I have hitherto depicted our situation in prose, I may now, perhaps, venture to give a poetical description thereof, in the shape of

### An Elegy

By a subaltern officer in cantonments on the banks of the Coa in 1811.

*In these dark, wretched, and unfurnish'd cells,*
*Where many a moping, half-starved hero dwells,*
*And ever-musing Melancholy reigns,*
*What mean these tumults in an ensign's veins?*
*Whence come these twitchings that invade repose?*
*Is it roast-beef, or shadows cross my nose,*
*Which, eager, snuffing up the tainted air,*
*Fancies it feasts on culinary fare?*
*Vain shadows, hence! nor dare to sport with one*
*So sad, so comfortless, so woe-begone,*
*Whose clamorous bowels cease to know good cheer—*
*Hunger in front, starvation in the rear.*
*Night's sable mantle now wraps nature up,*
*Now bucks to dinner go, and cits to sup;*
*Deep lost in sleep, around, my comrades snore,*
*Whilst I, awake, my adverse fate deplore;*
*Groan to the night's dull ear my lonely grief,*
*And sigh for England, and her fine roast-beef.*
*Oh! plenteous England, comfort's dwelling-place,*
*Blest be thy well-fed, glossy, John Bull face;*
*Blest be the land of aldermanic paunches,*
*Of rich soup turtle, glorious ven'son haunches!*
*Inoculated by mad martial ardour,*
*Why did I ever quit thy well-stored larder?*
*Why, fired with scarlet fever in ill time,*
*Come here to fight and starve in this curst clime?*
*In vision now I only feasts prepare,*

And, waking, feed like poets, on thin air.
My days lag tardily on leaden wings,
And night no comfort, no refreshment brings;
For though, oppress'd with toil, I seek for ease,
Nature's restorer flies from scoundrel fleas,
Who, e'en more num'rous than Arcadia's flocks,
Bite from my nightcap to my very socks,
And swarm all o'er, and thick infix their smarts,
As erst on Gulliver pour'd pigmy darts,
When fast by Lilliputian fetters bound,
He fumed, and swore, and bellow'd on the ground.
Now, while o'er all around uncertain sleep
Prevails, alone I my sad vigils keep,
Let me, like Philomel, pour forth my sorrow,—
The sad detail that fresh awaits tomorrow.
First, milkless tea presents the morn's repast,
Miscall'd a breakfast, but in truth a fast;
Harsh, mouldy biscuit, served in portions spare,
By niggard Commissary's frugal care;
No butter, no fresh eggs, no mutton-chops,
No crisp brown toast, such as spruce waiter pops,
In London coffee-house, beneath your beard,
When thrice the well-pull'd hungry bell is heard;
Not e'en a cup or saucer decks the board,
But from the haversack's foul motley hoard
A vessel's dragg'd, ten thousand debts to pay,
Doom'd to ten thousand uses, night and day.
Then dinner; oh, ye gods! who deign to stoop
To mortal's moans, contemplate this our soup.
See the smoking bullock's thin lean flanks,
Portion'd in morsels through the famish'd ranks;
See in camp kettles all we have to dine,
Yielding soup meagre that would frighten swine,
Such the two sorry meals—but two—alas!
And these scarce e'en enliven'd by a glass.
'Twere impious to insult the god of vines,

*Profane his sacred juice, his rosy wines,*
*By calling wine the rank, sour, scanty stuff,*
*Which "special favour" gives, nor gives enough,*
*Can such repasts be meant to feed and drench*
*Great Britain's heroes, sent to fight the French?*
*Better at home, in some dark cellar vile,*
*Mend shoes as cobbler, than starve here in style;*
*Or muffins cry, or occupation meek*
*Ply in St, Giles's, for a pound a week,*
*Ye fat rich citizens of London town,*
*Who roll in coaches, and who sleep in down,*
*Upraised by trade, who wallow in your wealth,*
*And snug o'er claret drink "the army's health,"*
*Turn here your eye, and give a pitying stare;*
*Come, and behold how we lank warriors fare,*
*Think not of ball-room strut, or lounging gait*
*In public walks, our military bait*
*To catch your daughters, oft ten-thousand prize,*
*Our gold and scarlet sparkling like their eyes;*
*But see the crimson'd coat seam'd o'er with stitches,*
*The torn, degen'rate, regimental breeches;*
*Behold how pale and worn the once brisk sash is,*
*See the last relics of these spatterdashes.*
*The ci-devant gay suit now altered grown,—*
*All glare, all brilliancy, all splendour gone.*
*Hail, sweet recruiting service! pleasing toil,*
*Ball-room campaigns, tea-parties, cards, dice, Hoyle:*
*Ye days when dangling was my only duty,*
*Envied by cits, caress'd by every beauty,*
*Dreaded by mothers, trembling at each glance*
*Shot at their daughters going down the dance.*
*Ah! how tormenting memory sad reviews*
*Those happy hours when in silk hose, thin shoes,*
*And sprightly scarlet, much the tailor's pride,*
*I lounged and flatter'd at the fair one's side!*
*Away, curs'd busy fancy; leave this vision;*

*Increase not misery by keen derision!*
*Away, quick hasten from these dreary walls;*
*Attend soft heroes to their plays and balls!*
*Pleasure's fled hence, wide now the gulf between us;*
*Stern Mars has routed Bacchus and sweet Venus.*

*I can no more; the lamp's last fading ray*
*Reminds me of parade ere break of day,*
*Where shiv'ring I must stand, though bleak the morning,*
*Roused by the drummer's hateful warning.*
*Come then, my boat-cloak, let me wrap thee round,*
*And snore in concert, stretch'd upon the ground,*
*Midst all these sleepers, grunting in their nooks;*
*Oh! may I dream of frying-pans and cooks,*
*Pots, spits, and larders, and when on viands fall,*
*Guzzle with aldermen of famed Guildhall.*
*And haste the day when I, on Albion's shore,*
*May stuff and cram till I can cram no more:*
*Haste the blest night when deep shall sink this frame*
*In fields of feathers, not in fields of fame.*

The above parody on Pope's *Abelard* came from Gallegos, the cantonments of the Light Division, and was printed by the perambulating press, established at head-quarters to facilitate the promulgation of Lord Wellington's orders. The few copies struck off fell amongst the personal friends of the author; some still living may recognize the attempt to turn privations into pleasantries, and to "laugh in care's face." These lines at the time obtained popularity and circulation without the aid even of booksellers or publishers.

It was the author of *The Pleasures of Hope*, I think, who said that he "forgave Buonaparte all his delinquencies, in consideration of his having, on one occasion, shot a bookseller." This remark surely ought to have come from the author of *The Pleasures of Memory*. I may say of the originator of the elegy, that while I leave to others the appreciation of the author's fancy, I reserve to myself a sure and lively remembrance of the truthfulness of the facts.

The bracing weather had the advantage of driving away my ague. In the absence of our Adjutant, who had departed on a visit to Lord Wellington, at head-quarters, his duties devolved upon me, which increased my occupations; nevertheless, I contrived to find time to take a gallop with another officer towards Ciudad Rodrigo, for the purpose of obtaining a sketch of the town and its environs. I passed our outposts, and proceeded three miles beyond them, as these only extended as far as the heights of Marialva, near Carpio.

We reached the enemy's *vedettes*, when they sent out a patrol after us, but I had accomplished what I wished before they made their approach. As in the state of the rivers nothing further could now be done with the enemy, we were put *en route* on the 30th of November for Navas, on our way to Pinhel, which we reached on the 1st of December. This town, though subjected to the frequent dilapidating occupation of the French, was a good quarter, not ill supplied with the requisites to render a sojourn there agreeable.

Sir Thomas Graham, and the head-quarter staff of our division, took up their abode in one of its chief houses; and we now began once more to use our best ingenuity to make our men's quarters comfortable and clean, and to strain our inventive faculties towards the same end, in favour of our own abodes. I luckily had, in common with a comrade, a quarter with the astounding luxury of glared windows to it: such palatial grandeur seldom in these days fell to the lot of a subaltern in that country; but we were not long destined thus to be framed and glazed.

The anticipatory idea of comfort was added to in no slight degree by the hospitality of the chief of our division[10], at whose table I frequently found myself a guest. However, "a change came o'er the spirit" of this dream, for I was shortly after sent out of town with my company to the Quinta de Toro, a mile and a half from Pinhel, on the road to Celorico. This had been a fine old *château*, the property of a Portuguese *Fidalgo*, who had fled

10. Sir Thomas Graham

147

on the French invasion. The enemy had done much damage, but there were still remaining some habitable rooms, with a great deal of fine old tapestry, and many other signs left of the better and happier days it had been witness to.

I know nothing more melancholy than to visit a fine old family mansion in a state of half-ruin; somehow I am apt, in my "mind's eye," to re-people it with its former occupants from generation to generation, and fancy all the youthful aspirations of hope, love, and kindly feelings that these chambers had encompassed in bygone days, mixed, no doubt, with fears, disappointments, anxieties, or distress, and "all the ills that man is heir to." To my mind there is something in the scenes of past pleasure or pain which sanctifies the spot where they have occurred.

Poor human nature had here played its high pranks; the chambers, with the broken remnants of furniture, bore silent testimony to all that once had been, but was no longer. Lodged in the *quinta* of a Portuguese noblemen, seated in a park, with the Coa's tributary streams running through it, surrounded with woods, and encompassed by walls, I began to fancy myself transmogrified into that *beau idéal* of English good taste—a country gentleman. The banished owner (and his "forbears," as they are called in Scotland) often came to my thoughts, although I knew them not, or ever did know them; even their names are now forgotten, although then familiar to me.

Foreign invasion had sent them forth wanderers from their hearths and home; they fled to Oporto, or elsewhere, rather than witness or expose themselves to personal insult or the ravages of war. Their forced absence was but an episode in such inroads on their country.

We found in these domains some game, and woodcocks in plenty, which afforded us not only the pleasure of exhilarating exercise, but a profit to our table.

This was too good to last. On the 17th I was sent, with a detachment of my regiment, on a working party, to the fortress of Almeida. This frontier stronghold was almost in a state of ruin; hardly a roof was left on any house. The French siege of it in

1810, the explosion of the magazine on that occasion, Brennier's destruction of the works on his abandoning the town in 1811, the precipitate mischief done by Packe on Marmont's advance against Spencer in the summer of the same year, rendered both the town and its fortifications a chaos. Two faces of the scarp and parapet of this hexagon-formed work (that to the west and south) had been blown into the ditch, and the guns buried in the ruins.

The works were now again undergoing repair, to place them in a state of sufficient defence against a *coup de main*. Our battering train had also arrived here, composed of seventy-eight heavy pieces of ordnance. A great number of cars were also in course of construction, to facilitate the conveyance of ammunition; and we were occupied in making fascines and gabions, and rapidly preparing, in every way possible, for carrying into effect the immediate siege of Ciudad Rodrigo.

The dilapidated state of Almeida, and the arrival of our heavy artillery, served as an excuse to the enemy for our operations, which they believed were confined merely to defensive measures of precaution, in preparing and arming this Portuguese frontier fortress.

Under this blind Lord Wellington put forth all his and our energies to hasten the preparations for the siege of the Spanish frontier fortress. The Light and Third Divisions were moved nearer to Ciudad Rodrigo; he called together all the general officers and heads of departments, not as a council, for he was not in the habit of asking other people's opinions on professional matters, but to give them his own. Having acquired the necessary information for himself, he admitted of no advice from others; he well digested and reflected on what he intended to accomplish, and, having made up his own mind, he laid down his instructions and gave his orders to carry them into effect, and on all possible occasions superintended their execution: he really was a chief on whom all depended.

What a contrast is this with Baron Müffling's descriptions of the councils of war, even within the Prussian army itself, in the campaigns of 1813 and 1814; the scenes described between himself, Gneisenau, and others, concerning the movements of their army; the open wrangling, coolnesses, jealousies, and differences in the Allied German Divisions of the same nation! How, with such a system and want of unity in command, they brought matters to the result they did, is surprising.

With us no time was lost in dispute or clashing opinions: one master mind prevailed throughout the whole of our campaigns; he thoroughly comprehended and taught others to execute that which he required. This was an immense advantage, and resulted (though frequently under most difficult circumstances) in entire success.

Being placed whilst at Almeida under the orders of the engineer officers, we lived entirely with them. After accomplishing our work we once more returned to Pinhel, and to our former country abode of the Quinta de Toro. A mail, —ay, news from England—dear old England!—a bundle of friendly letters awaited my arrival. No one but those who have experienced long delay and doubtful silence can sufficiently appreciate the pleasure derived from receiving in a distant land letters from home; circumstances at other times of small import then appear matters of deep interest; the slight indisposition of a friend, or the death of some favourite old dog, casts a deeper regret,—the success, health, or happiness, of those you love, bestows a greater pleasure.

In distance and uncertain absence the thoughtful minds and kind hearts whose affections guide their pens, afford invaluable testimonials to the longing recipients of them, particularly when one calculates the chance that they come from friends you "ne'er may see again." On again reaching my regiment I found that my comrades, in our absence, had been at work as well as ourselves, although not quite on the same objects.

Out of an old room they had constructed a theatre, and had got up amongst them the comedy of *The Heir at Law* while we of the working parties to Almeida had been preparing for *The Tragedy of the Siege and Capture of Ciudad Rodrigo.* The former intended theatrical representation was in a most untimely manner interrupted by the operations requisite for the latter. But before entering on a new year, or commencing another campaign, I may venture, in conclusion, to observe that this was begun on the 6th of March, and might be said to have closed in the December following; that Portugal had been completely liberated from French possession; and through numerous minor and two general actions and one siege Lord Wellington had established his army on a firm defensive footing on the northern frontier, holding the retaken fortress of Almeida, while Lord Hill's corps was left to cover the southern portion of that kingdom. In these manoeuvres and movements, of nine months' duration, our division had marched 849 English miles; without at all looking on such exercise as extraordinary, it was, at least, sufficient to keep our men in good wind, hardy condition, and sound understandings.

## CHAPTER 8

# Working in the Trenches

In September of 1811, after Marmont had relieved Ciudad Rodrigo, and subsequently replaced the cattle and Governor stolen from it by Julian Sanchez, the French Commander fell back to Salamanca, and eventually to Valladolid, with the greater part of his forces. "At this time also, 17,000 of the Imperial Guards were withdrawn by Napoleon for his Russian campaign, and above 40,000 troops of the enemy, of different arms, had quitted Spain on the same errand. The rest of their armies were spread over an immense extent of country. Marmont, deceived by the seemingly careless winter attitude of the Allies, and for the accommodation of provisioning his troops,"and watching the guerrilla corps, was at a greater distance from Ciudad than would enable him to assemble his army with facility to succour and support it on a sudden emergency; besides, his attention, at this time, was turned towards the operations going on in the east of Spain. Lord Wellington, well prepared, seized the opportunity he had long looked for; and, in spite of the inclemency of the season, suddenly and at once invested the fortress and commenced the siege.

It was at daybreak on a bitter cold morning, on the 4th of January, that our division started from their cantonments to take part in this siege, and commence the campaign of 1812. The Light, First, Third, and Fourth Divisions, with Packed Portuguese Brigade, were destined for this service, and were concentrated, in the first days of January, in the neighbourhood of our old battlefield, the banks of the Azava and Agueda. Across this latter river a bridge had been thrown at Marialva, by Lord Wellington.

Our first day's march, of sixteen miles, towards the scene of our new operations, was bad enough in respect to weather and roads; but, on reaching the half-roofless houses of As Navas, matters were still worse. He who had a soul for music might possibly view the creeks and crannies of our shelterless habitations with harmonious intentions, for many were the sites admirably adapted for the introduction of the Æolian harp; the less tasteful however, and the unmusical, who felt not the attributes of that which "soothes the savage breast" did not appear to have an adequate sense of the pleasures of their situation. In addition to other difficulties, we had to depend, for the transport of food, and all the requisite material for our operation, on our friends and allies, the Spaniards and Portuguese. The way in which this was accomplished is best shown by Lord Wellington's own words: in writing to Lord Liverpool, he says:—

What do you think of empty carts taking two days to go ten miles on a good road? After all, I am obliged to appear satisfied, or they would desert. At this season of the year, depending upon Portuguese and Spaniards for means of having what is required, I can scarce venture to calculate the time which this operation" (the siege) "will take; but I should think no less than twenty-four or twenty-five days. If we do not succeed, we shall, at least, bring back upon ourselves all the force that has marched away; and I hope we may save Valencia, or, at all events, afford more time to the Austrians and Galicians, etc. If we do succeed, we shall make a fine campaign in the spring.

On the 6th, head-quarters were moved to Gallegos. Lord Wellington, attended by Colonel Fletcher, Chief Engineer, and some officers of the staff, made a reconnoissance of the place; they crossed the Agueda by the fords about two miles below the town; and, unattended by any escort, reached several points from which they obtained a sufficient view of the defences (of the fortress) to decide on the attack[1]. Encased, but scarcely covered, we remained in a state of ventilation within the half-wrecked houses of As Navas till the 8th, when we joyfully moved to Espeja, as a village nearer to the scene of our future operations, and affording better shelter from the frost and snow. Toward sunset we reached the quarters intended for us during the siege; once ensconced in our different cottages, we refreshed ourselves with whatever provisions the commissary, our own industry, and a few dollars permitted us to obtain.

About eight o'clock p.m. we were contentedly sitting round a fire, in the full enjoyment of cigars and mulled wine, when a sound greeted our ears—not of Æolian chords, but the soldier's music—the cannon—booming forth through the calm frosty air of the night its sonorous eloquence. We went forth into the village street; the cannonade continued and became heavy; distance, and the wind in an adverse quarter, prevented our hearing any sound of musketry, but we saw, by the flashes from the guns, the horizon lighted far above the woods and undulating ground which intervened between our village of Espeja and the town of Ciudad.

A large assembly of officers and men were collected, in order to try to make out results from sound, but to little purpose beyond ascertaining that, as the cannonade continued throughout the night, the siege had begun. We thought that we should have had the honour of taking the initiative in this affair, but it was commenced by the Light Division in a clever, dashing style, and in the following manner.

Here, before inserting a farther quotation, let me plead my excuse for so doing. As often as I was not on the spot when some occurrence took place on which the subsequent narrative turns, I have left the relation of it to the authority either of an eye-witness or of the able historian of these campaigns; for, were I to describe what I did not see with my own eyes, I might be accused of presumption, and render myself liable to the rebuke

1. See Jones's *Sieges*.

which Hannibal conveyed when he happened to hear a distinguished orator discoursing on the subject of war. He was asked what he thought of it; Hannibal replied, *that he had heard many absurd things in his life, but never anything half so absurd as this.*

Would that some could recall to themselves the Italian proverb: *Chi non sa niente non dubita di niente!*

It would save many a controversy occasioning loss of valuable time and invaluable patience. But to return from this digression.

During the day, everything was kept as quiet as possible, and an equal examination made of every side of the town, so as to prevent any suspicion of an immediate effort, or of the point about to be attacked. The Light Division and Packers Portuguese Brigade forded the Agueda, near Caridad, three miles above the fortress; and, making a circuit, took post, without being observed, beyond the Tesso Grande, a round hill rising gradually from the city, on which the enemy had constructed a redoubt, (called after the abstracted Governor, Fort Renaud. This was distant from the fortified Convent of San Francisco four hundred yards, and some six hundred from the artillery on the ramparts of the place.)

The Light Division remained quiet during the day, unperceived by the enemy; and, as there was no regular investment, the enemy had no idea that the siege had commenced; but as soon as it became dark a brigade formed under arms on the northern side of the Upper Teson, and a working party of 700 men paraded in their rear, in two divisions of 300 men and 400 men respectively, the former intended to make a lodgement near the redoubt as soon as it should be carried, and the other to open a communication to it from the rear.

At eight p.m. Lieutenant-Colonel Colborne[2], with three companies of the 52nd Regiment, advanced along the

---

2. Now Lieutenant-General Lord Seaton.

Upper Teson to the assault of the redoubt. The garrison of the work discovered the assailants when about 150 yards distant, and had time to fire two or three rounds from their artillery (two guns and a howitzer) before the escalade commenced. Lieutenant Thomson of the engineers, who accompanied the detachment with a party of sappers, carrying scaling ladders, fascines, axes, etc., on arriving at the counterscarp, finding the palisades to be within three feet of it, and nearly of the same height, immediately placed the fascines from the one to the other, and formed a bridge by which a part of the storming party walked over the palisades, and jumped into the ditch, when, finding the scarp without a revetment, they readily scrambled to the top of the parapet, and came into contact with the bayonets of the defenders.

Whilst this was going forward in front, another party went round to the gorge, where there was no ditch, and forced over or through the gate; thus enveloped on every side, the resistance was short, and of fifty men, the garrison of the redoubt, four only escaped into the town, two officers and forty men being made prisoners, and three left dead in the work. The British loss was six men killed, and three officers and sixteen men wounded. Instantly the redoubt was carried, the precaution was taken of making its rear perfectly accessible, by breaking down the gates, and forming openings in its rear enclosure wall; but in a very short time the garrison directed such a quick fire into the work, that it was thought right to withdraw everyone from its interior.

The first division of workmen opened a trench on the flank of the redoubt as a lodgement, and the second division opened the communication to it from the rear across the Upper Teson, both of which operations were accomplished with little loss, as the garrison continued to direct nearly all their fire into the work throughout the night[3].

3. See Jones's *Sieges*.

Thus the Light Division commenced the siege. My friend Gurwood of the 52nd was of the party, and says:—

In my attempt to force the gate at the gorge we were interrupted by the enemy throwing over lighted grenades, but, as I saw the gate was low, I went round the angle of the fort, where I told Lieutenant-Colonel Colborne[4] that I thought, if I had a few ladders, I could get in at the gorge; the ladders were furnished, but were, however, of no use, for before they were placed the gate was suddenly blown open. I rushed into the fort, accompanied by Lieutenant Anderson of the 52nd and our men, and we met our other storming party coming over the angle of the redoubt.

On our return to camp I went to a shed in the rear, where, after receiving their wounds in the assault, Captain Mein and Lieutenant Woodgate of my regiment had been carried for the night, and where the lately-captured prisoners were also lodged until daylight. Here, in conversation with the French officer of the artillery, I learned the cause of the gate at the gorge of the redoubt being blown open, which had appeared so extraordinary to Lieutenant Anderson and myself. The French officer told me that a sergeant of artillery, in the act of throwing a live shell upon the storming party in the ditch, was shot dead, the lighted shell, falling within the fort; fearing the explosion of the shell among the men defending the parapet, he had kicked it toward the gorge, where, stopped by the bottom of the gate, it exploded and blew it open.

The successful night attack of the redoubt on the hill of San Francisco, otherwise called the Upper Teson, enabled our people immediately to break ground within six hundred yards of the place, notwithstanding the enemy still held the fortified convents flanking the works of the town. This was at once a great step gained in time and progress. The rise on which stood the captured redoubt was a plateau that extended towards the city,

---

4. The present Lord Seaton.

but suddenly descended to a valley and small stream.

On the opposite side of this, and within very commodious musket-range of the ramparts of the town, rose a small round eminence called the Lower Teson. The ground was rocky, and in some parts shingly, and the fire brought to bear on this attack by the enemy was greater than on some other points that might have been chosen; but Lord Wellington selected this in preference to any other, for he was fighting against time as well against the garrison, and wished to make short work of it, by taking the town before Marmont could possibly attempt to relieve it. On arriving at Espeja, on the evening of the 8th, our division had been ordered to cook a day's provisions overnight, for the next day's service.

On the morning of the 9th, in darkness, our battalions assembled for the purpose of relieving the Light Division. The noise of the city's guns still continued to disturb the calm of the night, and their echoes accompanied us as we moved from the cover of our village to take our share in the operations of the siege. From the assembled columns at our alarm post we broke into line of march, and about nine o'clock reached the ford of the Agueda. The river was partially frozen, and the stream rapid and deep, with much ice on the sides, and two or three feet depth of water in the shallows. Previous to our descent to take water, which our fellows did like good poodle-dogs who had something to bring out of it, the column was halted and orders received for our men to strip off their shoes and stockings.

On commencing the unusual operation of denuding their lower extremities, between two high banks in a close and narrow lane, we were made folly aware of the absence, in our neighbourhood, of Houbigant Chardin or any other dealer in perfumery. Our commander's act of consideration for the men, however, proved of no small comfort, as well as benefit to them, destined as they were to be exposed to atmospheric influences for twenty-four hours in a hard frost, and thus saved both their feet and their shoes.

Passing a second small stream, we arrived about midday in

rear of the Tesso Grande. This hill concealed our bivouac from the sight of the enemy's guns, and here were assembled the materials for the siege and the relief of the divisions destined to use them.

The German Legion were the first to relieve the working parties and guard of the trenches, previously occupied by the Light Division under Major-General Sir Robert Craufurd. Our predecessors had obtained for themselves a pretty good cover during the night; in the day our relieving parties were occupied in deepening, widening, and perfecting the approaches to the first parallel. The garrison threw a good many shells from heavy thirteen-inch mortars, and some round shot from the convent of San Francisco and the ramparts, but not with the effect or damage they intended, although the ground was hard from frost and flinty by nature, and the enemy's missiles were increased by driving the stones their shot encountered, like grape, amongst and over our men at work.

Soon after four p.m. our brigade relieved the Germans; we had a covering party of 500, and a working party of 1200 men. The enemy appeared already to have discovered the time fixed for our reliefs, being able to see, probably from the top of the cathedral, the movements on the plateau of the Tesso Grande. On entering the trenches they welcomed us with a pretty brisk cannonade and fire of shells, a species of cricket-ball that no one seemed in a hurry to catch; indeed, as an old cricketer, I may presume to say, that, fortunately, the "fielding" was most indifferent. No great mischief ensued, although some few casualties occurred; and we commenced working on the first parallel and intended batteries at one and the same time.

It snowed, and the night was intensely dark and cold; one of our comrades, a good-natured, agreeable little fellow, who sang beautifully, put on three shirts to preserve his voice, for which care of himself, though his appearance verged on the globular, we all felt sincerely obliged to him[5].

5. Many years have sped since then; I hear however that he still favours his intimate friends with the charms of his song.

159

As far as the fire from the ramparts could keep us warm, the enemy were considerate, both as to abundance and variety of fuel. They poured a very heavy shower on our trenches and our continuation of the first parallel, their calibre of gun being twenty-four and thirty-two pounders. They knew pretty well our intention to break fresh ground in the dark, and were uncomfortably curious to discover the exact spot of our operations.

During this work my observation was occasionally drawn to the features and general bearing of our soldiers; they seemed "as men on earnest business bent," stern, and not to be frustrated. The frequent cry of "shot!" or "shell[6]!" from men posted on the look-out, to warn us when such left the enemy's mortars, was very harassing. That of "shot" however was nearly unheeded, as the ball either passed, struck the outside of the trench, or knocked someone over, almost as soon as the cry was uttered. Our party were occupied in breaking ground, by placing gabions and filling them as fast as possible; we excavated the earth on the inner side, and thus covered ourselves as quickly as we could.

Captain Ross, the directing engineer of the night, a most intelligent and excellent officer, was killed by a round of grape from a gun on the convent of San Francisco, as he was in the act of giving us orders. Scarce a moment had elapsed before a sergeant of our detachment was knocked over by one of the stones that the round shot from the town scattered in all directions. Light-balls flew from the ramparts in frequent parabolas, shedding a red glare on all around, bright enough to indicate not only our points of operation, but the very forms of our men as they were working.

Thither the enemy directed their guns, and salvos of shot and shell immediately followed the discovery. While the glare of light lasted, the shower of missiles fell so thick in its vicinity that we were ordered to conceal ourselves till it was over. Then,

6. Thirteen-inch mortars threw into the air their iron balloons from the enemy's ramparts.

again emerging, we recommenced, like moles, to bury ourselves in the earth,—a curious expedient to avoid that ceremony at the hands of others.

The French, *par parenthèse*, doubtless imagined that, like Charles the Fifth, we were rehearsing our own funeral, and gradually inuring ourselves to being dead; many of us with a success ever more prompt than attended the apprenticeship of that hypochondriacal potentate. Although supperless, we worked throughout the night, actively and to the satisfaction of the engineering officers. We were anxiously looking out for dawn, which would test the worth of our night's exertions.

At last early light appeared in the east, streaking like a thread the sky above the mountains. An interesting panoramic view presented itself from our trenches on the Tesso Grande. The atmosphere was clear, frosty, and bracing; the surrounding scene bold and beautiful. In the centre of a large undulating plain, backed by broken ground, covered with ilex and cork-wood, stood the tall city, rearing its head over the surrounding level. The absence of foliage in its immediate vicinity caused the forms of the buildings to stand out in hard relief beneath the morning light.

The sun's young rays glanced on the cupolas of its churches and convents, and made the rising smoke from the city's early fires look still more blue. In the far distance were seen the snow-covered Sierras de Francia and de Gata warmly tinged by the sunlight, contrasting well with the silver-coloured stream of the Agueda. For a moment there was a dead calm, broken only by the occasional booming of a gun, fired as if in sleepy laziness, which perhaps the unusual activity of the previous night had engendered.

The sounds from the guns echoed through the pure thin air to the distant hills, bounding back again in threefold repetition of defiance; while in our front sternly stood the bold fortress flouting its hostile flag in the morning breeze. The cannonade was for the present confined to our opponents; as yet we made no response, but were merely preparing a reply; when the time did, come, our iron-tongued oratory was the most convincing, and prevailed.

After fourteen hours' occupation of the works, and having traced out the three batteries (Nos. 1, 2, and 3), we were relieved, and found the enemy as much *aux petits soins* for us as when we entered the trenches, dismissing us with all the honours of war. They blazed away with much noise, but to little purpose. Of our brigade, we lost, during the whole night's operations, not one officer, and only six rank-and-file killed and ten wounded. Colonel Fermor[7] of the Guards, the field officer commanding in the trenches, had his hat shot off by the splinter of a shell, which was the nearest approach to promotion in his corps during the night.

We reached our bivouac in rear of the Tesso Grande, where neither hut, tent, nor scarcely a fire was to be seen, there being a melancholy deficiency of material for such accommodation. Tents there were none, for not until the year after, in the campaign of 1813, were such save-health essentials issued out to our army[8]. We formed column and moved off in march from our barren place of assembly, to return once more to our country village quarters, judiciously using the same salutary precaution in repassing the streams we had adopted in fording them on our advance to the trenches. About four p.m. we again arrived at Espeja, and right glad we were to find ourselves under cover; for—

*Condisce i diletti*
*Memoria di pene,*
*Nè sà che sia bene*
*Chi mal non soffrì.*

---

7. Afterwards Lord Pomfret.

8. "Our own correspondent" in the *Times*, on the landing of our troops in the Crimea, expresses his astonishment that "old generals, young lords, and gentlemen" should bivouac and have "no bed but a reeking puddle, under a saturated blanket." From the year 1808 to that of 1813 our army were without tents; and many a night, in the four first campaigns in the Peninsula, and even the nights at Quatre Bras and before Waterloo, have these "old generals" experienced this unheard-of hardship.

Much to our satisfaction we here greeted Sanguinetti the sutler, that man of elastic views in moral and monetary obligations; he had reached our village from Lisbon, with a cargo of hams, porter, brandy, champagne, tea, cheese, and other comestibles, with which to warm the inward man and strengthen the body.

We now learned that the enemy had some 15,000 men upon the Upper Tormes, and that Marmont might be expected to make every possible exertion to relieve Ciudad Rodrigo from our attack. Still, we well knew the rapid and prompt action of our chief in anything he undertook, and with perfect confidence we awaited the result.

On the 11th, at daybreak, most part of our battering train from Almeida passed through Gallegos for the trenches on the Tesso Grande; and on the 13th we again moved towards the city, to resume our share of industry in accomplishing the batteries and advances of our works of attack. On our reoccupation of the trenches, we found progress had been made, but not so rapidly as could have been wished: the weather was so cold, and the enemy's fire so warm, that, in conjunction with the want of transport for the necessary materials, the labour had been greatly impeded; even the greater portion of ammunition for the battering train was still waiting conveyance from Villa de Ponte, and we again heard that Marmont was collecting his forces to succour the place.

Every exertion was used to complete the batteries, but the front they occupied was so very limited, and the garrison directing their fire against them only, had now attained the range so accurately, and threw shells so incessantly and with such long fuses, that half the time and attention of the 1000 workmen of our brigade were directed to self-preservation.

To oppose this heavy fire, it became necessary to persevere in making the parapets of the batteries of sufficient thickness; and all the excavation being confined to the interior, both night and day, the progress of the work was very unsatisfactory, particularly as, the batteries being on the slope of the hill, it required considerable height of parapet to secure their rear[9]. These causes induced Lord Wellington to change his plan; and he resolved to open a breach from his counter-batteries, which were from 500 to 600 yards distant from the curtain of the enemy's ramparts, and then storm the place without blowing in the counterscarp.

We found that during the night of the 12th, and early on the morning of the 13th, in a fog, which occasionally arose from the Agueda, the Light Division had dug pits beneath the walls of the city, in which the 95th Rifles were placed for the purpose of picking off the enemy's gunners, while too correctly and to us inconveniently serving their guns.

These pits were little separate excavations in the earth at some few yards' distance from each other, and about 150 from the enemy's embrasures. From our sloping eminence they looked like so many little graves, and had all the convenience of such, for, once arrived in them, the occupant was safe enough; but as neither sap nor cover of any kind assured the communication with such deadly holes, the great danger was in reaching these spots of interment, except under cover of fog or night.

From these counterfeit graves many of the enemy's gunners were put in preparation to inhabit real ones; that is, if any of their friends had sufficient delicate attention for them to take the time or trouble to dig them. During this night we again had sharp work from cold, labour, and our opponents' destructive intentions. A dropping fire of musketry from the ramparts continued to visit us, and two of my party at work on the parapet of No. 2 battery were hit, which, considering the distance (about 600 yards) and the darkness, was accidental, although looked upon by us, in those days of short ranges, as an extraordinary circumstance. The enemy's light-balls were constant, and their round shot and heavy thirteen-inch shells followed in abundance.

On one of these machines falling perhaps within a distance from us of only a few feet, the general order for immediate prostration was given, and it was curious from this posture to look

9. See *Jones* and *Napier*.

on our men's impatient faces while watching the hissing fuse, and awaiting its expected explosion, which generally covered those in the neighbourhood with dust and dirt; then up once more they were, and to work again like "good uns."

On passing down the trenches with Lieutenant Marshall of the Engineers[10], from whom I was receiving instructions for my portion of the working party, a shell alit close to us and immediately burst, carrying a splinter near to Marshall's head: he showed his disapprobation of such a liberty by impatiently exclaiming "Oh, you brute!" as if the cold projectile had had any choice in the course it had taken.

A simultaneous flight of these monsters was puzzling, as it rendered them difficult to avoid, and had not traverses been thrown up in the batteries, the casualties must have been much greater than they were. At first, these unwelcome visitors were regarded by us as no joke, but when accustomed to them, our men would laugh at the inconvenient accidents they occasioned; such as some fellow in the dark, in endeavouring to avoid one of these noisy intruders on our privacy, throwing himself into a spot more immediately handy than choice, and rising from his recumbent position adorned with the fortunate attributes of the Goddess Cloacina. One incident of this kind I well remember happened to poor Rodney of the Guards.

This night we got twenty-eight guns into the trenches, laid the platform, began the second parallel, and continued the approaches by the flying sap. The Santa Cruz Convent was surprised and stormed by the light infantry of the Germans of our division. This last success relieved us from a very ugly flanking fire, brought on our working parties from this most ecclesiastical habitation, and the right of the trenches was thus secured.

Some of the German officers suffered severely during the night's operations; one poor fellow, whose name time has obliterated from my memory, had both his legs carried off by a round shot. At three a.m. we were relieved, our brigade having made

---

10. Afterwards Lieutenant-Colonel Marshall, an energetic man and good soldier, who was wounded later in this siege.

good progress during our eleven hours' work. In the morning we once more took our road to Espeja, and again made our pedestrian ablutions in repassing the Agueda.

Restored to our village cabin-homes (for a soldier's home is wherever he may happen to sleep), and cordially greeted by the Spanish peasants, we indemnified ourselves for past fatigue, by rest and provender. When off duty in the trenches our parades were as regular as those in a garrison barrack-yard or "nigger" colony. B——, subaltern to the company next to mine, was a dry fellow, with considerable humour; his captain an old officer and brevet-major. Unlike Voltaire's description of *Le Père Adam, qui n'était pas le premier des hommes*[11], our major was an excellent man— father by seniority of us all, but prim, stiff, exceedingly correct in all he did or said, and with the best-brushed coat in the battalion.

These advantages obtained for him the sobriquet of the Parson; but this name, however well known to "the young ones," was too much revered ever to be breathed in presence of its possessor. The morning after our return from the trenches B—— was called over the coals for appearing late on parade.

As soon however as he had inspected, told off, and proved his company, he approached the group of officers assembled in the centre, and in the most solemn manner placed in the hands of the captain of his company its morning state, at the same time reporting to him, with the greatest gravity of countenance, that the congregation were in good order. The shouts of laughter which ensued compensated B—— for the previous rebuke to which he had exposed himself.

About four or five p. m. of the 14th, we heard the increased fire of artillery from the siege, and knew from it that the medicine we had been preparing overnight, was now in course of administration. We were also informed the following day, that a sortie had been made by the garrison, but was checked by the working parties in the trenches, who took to their arms and repulsed the attempt. In the evening our batteries opened: twenty-

11. A Jesuit, one of the standing butts of the lively philosopher.

five pieces were directed on the *fausse braie* and rampart, and two against the Convent of San Francisco.

Fifty pieces of cannon replied in hot haste to the opening of our guns, and the distant hills reverberated the hostile sound of eighty contending pieces of artillery. In the night, the other religious sanctuary of San Francisco was stormed, and taken by the 40th Regiment.

It would be tedious to recapitulate the same scenes which have already been described; suffice it to say, on the 17th our Division again took its turn of duty, and once more occupied the trenches. The only difference was, that our works now approached nearer to completion, and to the fated pity. Lord Wellington, who never procrastinated, had ordered a battery to be formed and armed, to create a smaller breach in a turret to the left of the larger one. The cannonade became sharper and more animated. We were no longer, as when last in the enemy's vicinity, the only objects acting as targets: the "reciprocity" now was not all on one side.

We laboured in repairing the batteries and platforms injured by the enemy's shot. The second parallel was pushed to the Lower Teson, within 180 yards of the ramparts: our defences were made higher as we descended the slope—firing parties were mixed with our workmen, to keep up an incessant discharge of musketry on the breach. The occupants of the little graves, as we called them, in spite of the infliction of showers of grape from the town, rendered good service. Still the garrison's shot knocked about our new-laid gabions, injured some of our guns in the batteries, wounded the commandant of our artillery, General Borthwick, and entirely ruined the sap, without the slightest regard to our taste or convenience.

The casualties of our division, however, were fortunately very few in proportion to the quantities of hard material flying about, and the weight of fire brought on our works. In the morning, in a fog, we left the trenches. During these duties a feat of gormandizing was performed by a soldier of the 3rd Guards. Vegetables were scarcely ever to be heard of, gardens hardly to be seen, and the constant visitation of this portion of the frontier provinces by four armies of different nations did not by any means assist horticultural pursuits, but rendered the produce of such industry in marvellous request. The Guardsman was on a piquet in a garden under the city walls, wherein he devoured so large a portion of raw cabbage, that, not having the stomach of a cow, he died, poor fellow! Others, stationed in the same paradise of an outpost, more prudent or less voracious, secured these rarities to carry off;

> *And, with sense more canny, and less savage,*
> *'took the liberty to boil' their cabbage.*

Considerable progress in achieving their object had been made by our breaching batteries; and again, as we dragged our slow length along towards our village shelter, we conversed on the chances of our division storming.

On the 20th we should again have charge of the trenches, and we trusted that by that day the breach would be practicable; and as we had had our share of the dirty work, we hopefully looked forward to obtain some of the honours. But in this we were unluckily disappointed.

On the 18th our fire was resumed with increased violence, and our guns were right well served.

On the 19th, Major Sturgeon[12] of the staff corps having closely examined the place, both breaches were reported practicable; our battering guns were then turned against the artillery of the ramparts, a plan of attack was formed, and Lord Wellington ordered the assault for that evening. The general order to accomplish his intent was issued in that direct, succinct, and terse language so peculiar to himself.

Head-quarters, Jan. 19th, 1812.

The attack upon Ciudad must be made this evening, at

---

12. Not he of the Mayor of Garret, who, with "Captain Tripe and Ensign Pattypan, returning to town in the Turnham Green stage, was stopped, robbed, and cruelly beaten by a single footpad." This Sturgeon was a different guess kind of character. He was unfortunately killed by a French *tirailleur* in the south of France, in 1813, while reconnoitring from a vineyard some of the enemy's columns.

seven o'clock;

Which sounded very much like, "the town of Ciudad must be taken this evening, at seven o'clock." The assault occurred under the eye and immediate superintendence of Lord Wellington. In giving a sketch of the storming of the town, I shall confine myself to some few details drawn from memoranda of my own made at the time, information obtained from others, actors in the scene, and a pamphlet printed for private circulation, but not published, given to me by my friend Gurwood, who led the forlorn hope at the little breach.

The operation of the assault was confided to the Third Division under Picton, who was charged with the right and centre attack, and that of the great breach; the Light Division under Craufurd, with the left attack on the small breach; and Packers Portuguese, with a false attack on the reverse side of the town. As soon as it was dark, the Third Division was formed in the first parallel, the Light Division behind the convent of San Francisco, and the Portuguese Brigade on the Agueda, above the bridge.

They all "in silent muster and with noiseless march" moved simultaneously to the posts allotted them. Hay-bags, hatchets, and scaling-ladders were provided and distributed to each advance party according to the requirements of their respective services. The right attack was led by Colonel O'Toole, of the Portuguese Caçadores; the centre, to the great breach, by Major Manners of the 74th, with a forlorn hope under Lieutenant Mackie of the 88th; the left was commanded by-Major Napier of the 52nd, with a forlorn hope under Lieutenant Gurwood of the same regiment. The advance or storming parties were composed,' both men and officers, of volunteers: the number being limited, the selection of the candidates for this service created amongst the rejected great jealousy and discontent.

All the troops reached their posts without seeming to have attracted the enemy's attention[13]. Lord Wellington, who had been reconnoitring the breaches in the ramparts, was standing

---

13. Gurwood.

on the top of the ruins of the convent of San Francisco, and in person pointed out the lesser breach to Colonel Colborne and Major Napier; he addressed the latter by saying, "Now do you understand exactly the way you are to take, so as to arrive at the breach without noise or confusion?"

Napier's answer was, "Yes, perfectly,"

Some of the staff observed to Napier, "Why don't you load?"

He replied, "No; if we cannot do the business without loading, we shall not do it at all."

Lord Wellington instantly turned round, and exclaimed, "Leave him alone!"

Craufurd, on all occasions of this nature, like some Greek hero or Roman leader, was much given to eloquence, and always addressed to his division a speech. It was his usual way, and was more a habit of his own than one requisite to such men and officers as composed the Light Division: they would have done his bidding and their duty at a simple word of command. The general not speaking Portuguese, called upon Lieutenant-Colonel Elder[14], commanding the 3rd or Villa Real Caçadores of the Light Division, to address some expressions of encouragement to his men. Elder, though in command of a corps of that nation's troops, unfortunately was as innocent of the vernacular of their language as the general himself; Elder's powers of speech, even in his own tongue, did not run to seed or into anything at all approaching to the oratorical or classical: more prompt in deed than word, he conveyed his communications to his corps in a kind of Anglo-Portuguese, or rather Portuguese English, a species of *lingua franca* peculiar to himself, but which they understood.

His men admired his courage, liked his conduct, and would have followed him anywhere and everywhere. It is but justice to this officer to say that his battalion was in the very best possible state of discipline, and set an example advantageous for other corps to follow. At this moment the firing commenced on the

---

14. Afterwards Major-General Sir George Elder.

right with the Third Division. Craufurd again impatiently called out, "D— it, Sir, why do you not obey my orders and speak energetically to your men?"

Elder was puzzled, and at last he roared out, "*Vamos, Villa Real!*" which was about one of the greatest efforts at eloquence he had ever attempted in his life in any language. But it was effective. Elder's people were destined to carry hay-bags to throw into the ditch to lessen the depth for the men to jump down; but as some delay and mistake occurred in their delivery to the Caçadores, the signal to advance was given in the meantime. Away went the storming party of three hundred volunteers under Major Napier, with a forlorn hope of twenty-five under Gurwood: they had about three hundred yards to clear before reaching the ditch of the town: these troops at once jumped in, the *fausse braie* in the centre was scaled, and the foot of the breach was gained; but the ditch being dark and intricate, Gurwood at first led his party too much to the left, and missed the entrance to the breach, but placed his ladders against the wall of the *fausse braie*, and thus taking in flank the enemy, who were defending it, they hastily retired up the breach.

The other stormers went straight to their point. At this moment the leader of the forlorn hope was struck down by a wound in the head, but sprang up again and joined Major Napier and Captain Jones of the 52nd, together with Captain Mitchel of the 95th Rifles, Ferguson of the 43rd, and some other officers, who, at the head of the stormers, were all going up the breach together. When two-thirds of the ascent had been gained, the way was found so contracted, with a gun placed lengthways across the top, which closed the opening, that our leading men, crushed together by its narrowness towards the summit, staggered under their own efforts and the enemy's fire.

Such is the instinct of self-defence, that, although no man had been allowed to load, every musket in the crowd on the breach was snapped. At this moment Major Napier was knocked down by a grape-shot, which shattered his arm. In falling, he was supported by Lord March, *aide-de-camp* to Lord Wellington, who from impulse had gone with the storming party into the ditch, but he called to his men to trust to their bayonets. All the officers simultaneously sprang to the front, when the charge was renewed with a furious shout, and the entrance was gained.

The supporting regiments followed close, and came up in sections abreast: Lieutenant-Colonel Colborne, although very badly wounded in the shoulder, formed the 52nd on the top of the rampart, wheeled them to the left, and led them against the enemy. The 43rd went to the right, and the place was won. During this contest, which lasted only a few minutes after the *fausse braie* was passed, the fighting continued at the great breach with unabated violence; but when the 43rd and the stormers came pouring down upon the enemy's flank, the latter bent before the storm.

Picton's Division carried the great breach after innumerable obstacles and a continued smashing fire from the enemy. Packe, with his Portuguese Brigade, converted his false attack into a real one; and his leading parties under Major Lynch followed the enemy's troops from their advance works into the *fausse braie*, and made prisoners of all who opposed them.

All the attacks having succeeded, "in less than half an hour from the time the assault commenced our troops were in possession, and formed on the ramparts of the place, each body contiguous to the other; the enemy then submitted, having sustained considerable loss in the contest[15]."

Unlike Baillie Nichol Jarvie's description of "fellows that would stick at nothing," our fellows stuck at everything they met. High stone walls, well-defended ramparts bristling with musketry, mines, loop-holed houses, live shells, and grape-shot, are irritating obstacles, and likely to create delay to forward movements. It is difficult, in storming a town on a dark night, to know exactly the moment when resistance really ceases and forbearance should begin.

The very nature of this kind of service gives great license to dispersed combatants to form their own peculiar opinions

15. See *Duke of Wellington's Despatches.*

on this very delicate subject. In such moments of excitement, individual responsibility becomes great, and the decent duties of forbearance are too frequently apt to be thrown aside in favour of settling all doubts by the bayonet. Our division not having *assisté,* as the French call it, in the storming, I shall continue to give its details as they came to my knowledge from those who were present. I will now, therefore, more at large allow my friend Gurwood to tell his own story of the assault of the place and the surrender of its Governor.

On leaving the bastion, to go along the rampart to the left, my attention was attracted by a cry; and I saw some soldiers of my party, one of whom was Pat Lowe, in the act of bayoneting a French officer who resisted being plundered. Having lost my sword in the breach when stunned, I picked up on the rampart a broken French musket, knocked Lowe down, and saved the French officer, who complained to me of being robbed of his epaulette or something else. I told him that he might think himself lucky, after the garrison had stood an assault, to have his life saved. I said I would protect him, but that he must accompany me to the Salamanca gate, which I knew to be close at hand.

He said it was useless to attempt to open it, as it was *murée*—blocked up with stones. I went down, however, by one of the slopes from the rampart to examine, and found it as stated. On questioning the French officer where he thought the Governor might be, he told me, that previous to assault, he had been seen going in the direction of the great breach, but that, if not killed, he would no doubt be found either in his house or at *La Tour Quarrée,* or citadel. The ramparts were filled with men of the Light Division descending into the town.

On passing over the gate of San Palayo I saw from the wall a large party of French in the ravelin of the *fausse braie* outside, crying out that they had surrendered; but we could not get at them. We then heard an explosion, and, from the smoke, saw it was in the direction of the great breach. This explosion was followed by a dead silence for some moments, when it was interrupted by the bugles of the regiments of the Light Division sounding 'Cease firing.' I was thus assured that all was safe. I continued along the ramparts until we arrived at the citadel or *Tour Quarrée*, which commanded the bridge over the river.

The gate was closed. M'Intyre, one of the men with me, proposed blowing the gate open by firing into the lock; but on seeing some of the enemy on the top of the turrets of the tower, and at the recommendation of the French officer who was with me, I went round from the gate to the rampart, from whence I called out to them to surrender, or they would be put to death, as the town was taken.

The answer being to return to the gate, which would be opened, I did so and found admittance. I proceeded with the person who opened it to the square tower inside, the door of which was closed. The officer who had opened the outside gate, told me that the Governor and other officers were within the Tower. I repeated the threat, that they would certainly be put to death if they did not surrender, but that I would protect them if they did. I was answered from within, "*Je ne me rendrai qu'au Général en Chef.*"

I replied that the *Général en Chef* would not take the trouble to come there, and that if the door was not immediately opened it would be blown open, '*qu'ils périraient tous.*' After some slight hesitation, the door was unbarred, and I found my way in with Corporal M'Intyre and Lowe behind me. It was a square chamber, and, as I saw by the light of a lantern held up by one of them, filled with officers. The lantern was immediately knocked down by a musket from behind me, and Lowe, who did it, cried out, 'Dear Mr. Gurwood, they will murder you.' All was now dark, excepting from the light of the moon, then rising and shining through the open door from behind us.

I was seized round the neck, and I fully expected a sword in my body; but my alarm ceased immediately on the person kissing me, saying, '*Je suis le Gouverneur de la place, le Général Barrié; je suis votre prisonnie.*' He then took off his sword and gave it me. I received it, telling him that I would take him to the *Général en Chef*, to whom he should surrender his sword. I conducted him out of the tower, saying that I would protect any of the officers who chose to accompany me. I told M'Intyre and Lowe that I no longer required them, and I descended with my prisoners from the Tower into the town, proceeding by the main street, which led from the bridge to the Plaza Mayor. There was still some firing going on, but chiefly from plunderers blowing open the doors of houses, by applying their muskets to the Jocks.

At the request of the Governor I proceeded to his house in the *Plaza*. The troops were pouring in on all sides, most of them of the Third Division. I called out, as I went, for Lord Wellington, when a gruff and imperious voice, which I knew to be that of General Picton, said, 'What do you want with Lord Wellington, Sir? you had better join your regiment.'

Fearing to lose my prisoners, I made no reply, but having ascertained, while in the Governor's house, from Captain Rice Jones, of the Engineers, that Lord Wellington was coming into town from the suburb of San Francisco by the little breach, I followed that direction. On leaving the Plaza Mayor, and when out of hearing of General Picton, I continued crying out, 'Lord Wellington! Lord Wellington!' In the care and protection of my prisoners I necessarily overlooked and abandoned many things, and heeded not the excesses I witnessed in my passage through the town; and on arriving at that part of the rampart in the vicinity of the little breach, I again cried out, 'Lord Wellington!' When a voice, which I recognized, exclaimed, 'Who wants me?' I immediately proceeded up the slope near the rampart; I crossed the trench with the Governor, the officer commanding the artillery, and three or four other officers, and I presented to Lord Wellington the Governor, to whom I gave back his sword, which I had carried since his surrender. Lord Wellington immediately said to me, 'Did you take him?'

I replied, 'Yes, Sir, I took him in the citadel above the Almeida gate.'

Upon which, giving the sword to me, he said, 'Take it, you are the proper person to wear it.'

The rising moon, and some few houses on fire near the little breach, rendered everything around visible. Lord Wellington, turning to Colonel Barnard[16] (of the 95th Rifles), said, 'Barnard, as Generals Craufurd and Vandeleur are wounded, you command the Light Division; you command in the town,—have it evacuated immediately.'

Lord Wellington then spoke to the Governor and the officer of the French artillery, respecting the gates and magazines, and gave other directions, at which moment Marshal Beresford asked me what was going on in the town; and on my telling him of the plunder and excesses I had witnessed on my passage through it, he repeated this to Lord Wellington. General Barrie interrupted them; on which Lord Wellington turned round to his *aide-de-camp* Lord Clinton, and said, 'Take him away.'

Seeing the Governor looking very much cast down, I was in the act of giving him back his sword, when the Prince of Orange[17] or Lord March[18] pulled me by the skirt of my jacket, and one of them, I believe Lord March, said, 'Don't be such a —— fool!

---

16. Now Lieutenant-General Sir Andrew Barnard, Deputy Governor of Chelsea.
17. Late King of the Netherlands.
18. Now Duke of Richmond.

CHAPTER 9

# Spanish Bigotry

Shortly after the surrender of the Governor, Lieutenant-Colonel Colborne, of the 52nd, came from the interior of the town to the lesser breach, and, being badly wounded, was helped over it by Lord Wellington's *aide-de-camp*, Captain Burgh[1] The confusion caused by a triumphant soldiery in a town taken by assault, and the excesses resulting from it, are more lamentable than surprising. In such events the definition between right and wrong is sadly mixed up, and I fear no distinction was made between our Spanish friends and our French enemies; at all events, it was not too nicely kept. The officers lost all control over their men. Alas! as Byron has it,—

*Sweet is*
*Pillage to soldiers, prize-money to seamen.*

The 43rd, under Lieutenant-Colonel Macleod[2], were amongst the best conducted; and in the surrounding hurly-burly, Captain Duffy's[3] company of that corps was remarked by Lord Wellington himself for its good discipline and soldierlike conduct. The French garrison originally consisted of about 2000 men, of which 300 had fallen during the siege, and 1700 men with 78 officers were made prisoners; 150 pieces of artillery, including the whole of the battering train of Marmont's army, were taken. The loss on our side, exclusive of him who killed himself by eat-

1. Now Lieutenant-General Lord Downes.
2. Killed subsequently at the storming of Badajoz.
3. Now Major-General Duffy.

177

ing cold cabbage in a garden, was 1200 men and ninety officers; 650 of the former and sixty of the latter were slain or wounded in the assault.

General Craufurd, a man of hot and eccentric temperament, but of great ability, was killed: he was shot through the lungs, and was buried on the 25th, on the spot where he received his death-wound, at the foot of the lesser breach. His remains were attended to their last home by Lord Wellington and his staff. General Mackinnon was killed by the explosion of the mine to which Gurwood's *Narrative* alludes, while leading his brigade in the Third Division; he was, with many others, blown from the top of the great breach into the ditch.

> This entrance into the city was cut off from it by a per-pendicular descent of sixteen feet, and the bottom was planted with sharp spikes, and strewn with live shells; the houses behind were all loopholed, and garnished with musketeers, and on the flanks there were cuts, not indeed very deep or wide, and the French had left the temporary bridges over them; but behind were parapets, so powerfully defended, that it was said the Third Division could never have carried them had not the Light Division taken the enemy in flank,—an assertion easier made than proved[4].

Mackinnon was a good and gallant soldier, and an intelligent man. He commanded a brigade in Picton's Division, although he regimentally belonged to the Coldstream Guards. With these perished many other fine fellows: amongst them a captain of the 45th, of whom it has been felicitously said, that "Three generals and sixty other officers had fallen, but the soldiers, fresh from the strife, only talked of Hardyman."

General Vandeleur, Colonel Colborne, and a crowd of infe-rior rank were wounded. Unhappily, the slaughter did not end with the assault: for the next day, as the prisoners and their escort were marching out of the breach, an accidental explosion took place, and numbers of both were blown into the air[5].

4. See *Napier*.
5. *Ibid.*

A curious statistic of the mass of fire brought by the enemy on our troops, during the siege of eleven days, from forty-eight pieces of ordnance, is given in Jones's *Sieges in Spain*. He states that 21,000 rounds of shell and shot were launched against our approaches. Confined as these were in space, and narrow in dimensions, it was astonishing, from the concentrated direction of the missiles, that our casualties were not greater.

Now, supposing all these to have occurred from the cannonade only, which was very far from being the case, and transferring the cause of loss of those who fell on this occasion from musketry, the bayonet, and mines, to the enemy's artillery alone, we should then have some five men killed or wounded for about every hundred rounds of cannon-shot and shell fired. From the above circumstance, I may be allowed to state to the uninitiated, how much more numerically destructive is the fire of musketry than that of round shot and shell.

In confirmation of this, I will here recite the following remarks made on the subject by other authorities.

At Cambrai, in 1817, at dinner at the Duke of Wellington's, I heard Sir George Wood[6] state, that in Lord Howe's great action on the 1st of June, two barrels and a half of gunpowder were fired for every man killed or wounded. "Ay," said the Duke, taking up the conversation, "and at Trafalgar, where about 25,000 British sailors were engaged, under 1300 were killed and wounded; while at Talavera de la Reyna, out of an army of 19,000 men I lost 5000, principally by musketry."

The Duke, whose economy in action of the life of his troops was well known to us, merely meant to state a simple fact in illustration of the effects of the different species of fire. He hated a "butcher's bill," and never made one if he could possibly avoid it, To quote his own words, in writing to one relative of one of his personal staff who fell at Waterloo, speaking of the victory gained, he says, "The glory resulting from such actions, so dearly bought, is no consolation to me"

6. Colonel Sir George Wood, then Chief of Artillery to the Army of Occupation in France.

Amongst other random recollections I noted the above conversation at the time. It is more forcibly brought to my mind by a feat of endurance of fatigue which I performed at the same period. I had reached Cambrai at a quarter past two p.m. that day, with despatches for the Duke from our Ambassador Lord Stuart de Rothesay, at Paris. I quitted the Embassy at half-past three the same morning, after a ball; was in my saddle by four, and rode the distance of twenty-two French *posts* (or 110 English miles), *franc étrier,* in ten hours and a quarter; delivered my despatches; dined at head-quarters, by the Duke's invitation; attended that night another ball at the Hôtel de Ville; had an early field-day the following morning; played a cricket-match against the garrison of Valenciennes, succeeded in getting fifty runs; attended a lively dinner under a tent, which somehow or other lasted till sunrise the following day, and was, after all, fresh and fit for duty as if I had done nothing. From the example of energy of mind and activity of body set us by our great chief, we were all, from spirit, training, and emulation, ready for and up to anything by night or day, in "camp, or court, or grove."

In a service short and sharp as that of the siege and capture of Ciudad Rodrigo, more than an ordinary amount of casualties must be expected, especially when we reflect that it was taken in eleven, instead of twenty-four days, the time originally contemplated as necessary by Wellington himself. Massena, previous to his attack on Portugal in 1810, took six weeks to plant the French flag on the city's ramparts. Our chief, not having had leisure to attend to the elementary procrastination of scientific engineering by which lives are saved, at once cut the Gordian knot which want of time did not allow him to untie.

Within four days' march of 45,000 Frenchmen under one of their most celebrated marshals, and against the strict rules of military science, he fairly wrenched the fortress from the enemy's grasp, and seized the prize. The bridge over the Agueda had been established only on the 1st of January, the trenches were opened on the 8th, and the city fell on the 19th. Marmont only heard of the attack on the 15th, and not till the 26th did he know of the capture of the fortress. On the first intelligence reaching him, he concentrated his army at Salamanca; but, on being made aware of his loss, he again retired to Valladolid. The theft was complete: Julian Sanchez, with the Austrian Strenuwitz, in our Hanoverian Hussars, had the previous autumn filched from the fortress its former Governor Renaud; and now our great chief had committed something more than petty larceny, by taking the town itself.

To recompense an exploit so boldly undertaken and so gloriously finished, Lord Wellington was created Duke of Ciudad Rodrigo by the Spaniards, Earl of Wellington by the English, and Marquis of Torres Vedras by the Portuguese. This last title was most certainly conquered long before it was surrendered by the Portuguese Government.

> Taking all the difficulties and peculiarities of the enterprise into consideration, the reduction of this fortress, whether viewed in conception or arrangement or execution, must be ranked as one of the happiest, boldest, and most creditable achievements recorded in our military annals[7].

None, certainly, could have accomplished the service better than those who took the town; still the regret in our division was great that we had not participated in the assault. One day later, and it would have fallen to our turn. We were almost tempted to blame the prompt decision of our chief. We had undergone all the unpleasant part—the dirty work and its attendant hardships—without obtaining any credit beyond preparing, in stealthy mole-like manner, the way for others to distinguish themselves.

When the distance we had to march, the icy streams we had to ford, the bivouacking in frost and snow without fire, the fatigue of labour and absence of rest every fourth day for thirty-five consecutive hours, were considered, we fairly might be allowed to envy those who, although participators in similar fatigue and privation, had at least gained the honours and rewards to which

---

7. See Jones's *Sieges*

their dashing gallantry had so fully entitled them. But, as there is no pleasing everybody, we were obliged to take things as they came: we grinned and bore it.

The day after the storming, I was sent in command of a party from Espeja to Ciudad, to recover, if possible, the body of General Mackinnon. We were some time in the search before we could discover his remains. After exhuming from fragments of masonry and dust many poor fellows' corpses, we at last extracted the general's from beneath others in the ditch, and it was conveyed by a sergeant's party to Espeja. Thinking that some memorial of him would be acceptable to his family, I remember cutting off from the back of his head a lock of hair, to send to his widow. I gave it to his friend and brother officer[8], Lieutenant-Colonel Jackson, deputy quarter-master of our division.

At Ciudad I found the Fifth Division had been brought up, and were in possession of the town, In the 4th Regiment, belonging to this division, was my friend Captain Burke, who gave me provender and a shake-down in his quarters for the night. They were all hard at work, levelling our trenches and destroying: our batteries; and the artillery of the battering train were withdrawing our guns and conveying them across the Agueda. Lord Wellington had been early into the town that morning, and, after examining the state of the defences, gave all the necessary orders for clearing away the rubbish from the breaches, and repairing the ramparts; after which he returned to Gallegos, and sent off his *aide-de-camp* (Captain Gordon of the Guards) the same day to England, with despatches reporting the capture of the place. Every arrangement was now made to restore the fortifications and provision the place quickly, as Marmont's army was expected. In anticipation of such an arrival, Hill's corps had been previously ordered up from the Alemtejo as far as Castello Branco.

On the 23rd we buried General Mackinnon with military honours. He was an amiable man, a good officer, and was much

---

8. Of the Coldstream Guards, afterwards Lieutenant-General Sir Richard Jackson, Commander-in-Chief in Canada.

regretted. His last place of rest was dug in the market-place of the small village of Espeja, and his remains were followed to the grave by his brother officers of the Guards.

It was strange, but true, that even after the recent services rendered by us to the Spanish nation, and with some claims to consideration, acknowledged at least by the peasantry, still priestly bigotry prevailed, and denied interment in consecrated ground to the remains of those "heretics" who had fought and fallen in their cause. We were regarded by them as quite fit to supply them with money, furnish them with munitions of war, and shield them from defeat in this world, but as by no means worthy of Christian burial, or our souls being saved in the next. The Turk is more tolerant.

As soldiers, this want of charity affected us but little: we viewed it more in pity than in anger. It was annoying to us only as wounding the feelings of the absent relations of those of our countrymen who fell. The Spanish nation might have been a little more courteous; and as we had come to be killed for their advantage, it would have been a little more civil had they allowed us to bury ourselves with due decency. We were however by no means particular on this point, having a decided preference for living in a good place, rather than coveting the pleasure of being buried in the choicest spot with the greatest distinction.

The rains, with strong gales of wind, now set in with such violence as only those can conceive who know what southern rains are. The trestle-bridge at Marialva was carried away, and the river rose two feet over the stone bridge under the walls of Ciudad; thus communications by roads were impeded, and the passage of the Agueda stopped. Had this occurred earlier, we should never have accomplished, as we did, the work of the approaches. Our trenches would have become aqueducts instead of viaducts, such as later we had some experience of at Burgos.

Frost acted on this occasion more efficiently as our ally than our friends the Spaniards. It was well known to us how often military operations are dependent on that which influences the barometer. The bad weather had its inconveniences even under cover of our village cabins.

One of them, in which lay part of my company, was either rained or blown down in the night, and several of the men were severely hurt; amongst them my Irish friend M'Culloch, famed, as I before mentioned, for more courage than arithmetic, not having been born to interfere with Babbage in his discovery of the calculating machine. The beam of the house fell on him and broke his arm, and he was otherwise so much injured as to oblige us to send him to the *depôt*-hospital at Coimbra, where the poor fellow died.

At this time I was again urged to return home. This word sounded warmly and cheerily in my ears. My news informed me of the death of a very near relative, the possessor of considerable landed property, to which my friends were good enough to suppose I ought to succeed; and they wrote under this impression, pressing my return to England to attend the opening of the will. There were few with us who would not have done their best to gain the estimation of him who commanded our army.

We well knew the high feelings by which he was actuated, and how he appreciated, from the lowest to the highest, those whom he found always ready and at all times in the right place. We were equally aware how our chief detested applications for leave, or excuses that took officers from their duty, and he frequently expressed his astonishment at the applications made to him for this purpose. I therefore replied to my friends (and I name this as a working of the spirit that had been instilled into and prevailed amongst us) that "if even —— has left me the family estate" which he did prospectively, "nothing will persuade me to quit the service or leave this army to go home until, in course of duty, I am ordered so to do."

Our army was drawn from the sinews of the people, the intelligence of the middle classes, and the scions of the titled and untitled landed aristocracy of our country, embodied together in arms to serve their fatherland. All, from the private soldier upwards, emulated obtaining the notice and meriting the good opinion of him who kept up the energies and inspired ardour into the hearts of those he commanded.

Great personal sacrifices were frequently made; ease, luxury, and independence were cast aside. In speaking, not only of that army, but of the profession in general, I cannot resist quoting here a well-merited and truthful paragraph from a letter recently published by the clever but eccentric member for Surrey, Henry Drummond, Esq., who, in relation to classes, and in assigning his reasons for declining to attend the Peace Conference lately held at Edinburgh, says:

> Take the army and navy as a class, and take any other class of men in the country; compare them together for talents, patriotism, honour, virtue, disinterestedness, kindness, self-devotion,—in short, every quality that ennobles men, and I assert that the military class is beyond measure superior to every other.

Here is a picture drawn by a disinterested observer; a man of acuteness, and great knowledge and experience of the world. From a life's service in the class alluded to, I may venture to bear testimony to the above view being just and true[9]. One of the causes which maintain high feeling and character in the profession of arms is, that when we do meet with an unworthy member of it, we get rid of him, whilst some other classes keep theirs, and not only occasionally try to defend them, but show great sensitiveness even when they are attacked: surely this is doing a wrong toward themselves. Why not use a little "fullers' earth" to take the stains out of their own cloth, as promptly and effectively as we do out of ours ? It is their bounden duty to cleanse themselves from suspicion, or they must submit with good grace to the chance and inconvenience of being condemned, perhaps unjustly, as a body, in public opinion.

But to return to our movements. In consequence of Marmont's threatened advance, we were kept on the *qui vive*. The

---

9. In exemplification of a sense of duty, patriotism and self-devotion, I cannot do better than refer to Captain M'Clure's late despatch to the Admiralty, on his discovery of the North-West Passage; it is fall of high-toned and right feeling.

report of his intentions was rendered still more suspicious by the floods having cut us off from communications with Ciudad Rodrigo. We feared the enemy might pounce upon the fortress before the fortifications had been sufficiently repaired, or that we could get at him. We consequently were ordered always to have a day's provisions cooked in advance, with which to line our haversacks, that we might be ready to move at a moment's notice; but this alert turned out to be unnecessary.

Our chief had no sooner succeeded in the capture and repair of Ciudad, and garrisoned it from the Spanish army under Castanos, its new Governor being Vives, to whom he personally gave instructions concerning the plan and intention of the new works and their defence, than he immediately turned his attention to attack Badajoz, and wrote, under date of the 29th, from Gallegos, to Lord Liverpool as follows:—

I now propose to attack Badajoz as soon as I can; I have ordered all the preparatory arrangements to be made, and I hope that everything will be in readiness to enable me to invest the place by the second week in March. We shall have great advantages by making the attack so early, if the weather will allow of it.

First, all the torrents in this part of the country are then full, so that we may assemble nearly our whole army on the Guadiana without risk to anything valuable here.

Secondly, it will be convenient to assemble our army at an early period in Estremadura for the sake of the green forage, which comes in earlier to the south than here.

Thirdly, we shall have advantages in point of subsistence over the enemy at that season, which we should not have at a later period. Fourthly, their operations will necessarily be confined by the swelling of the rivers in that part as well as here. The bad weather which we must expect, or other circumstances, may however prevent us from carrying our plan into execution; but I can only assure you that I shall not abandon it lightly, and I have taken measures to have the best equipments for this enterprise.

In consequence of this, we were all, with the exception of the Fifth Division, who remained on the frontier and in observation in the neighbourhood of Ciudad, put in movement for the Alemtejo. Our division's march was directed on Abrantes, for the purpose of reclothing our fellows; with which object the clothing had been sent up to that town from Lisbon,—it must be confessed, not before it was wanted, for in the haberdashery line we were all a little like those troops with which Falstaff, from a delicate sense of propriety, would not march through Coventry. The captain of my company having gone home on leave, I once more tumbled into the command of it.

On the occasion of our march to the south, my horse being "a galled jade, whose withers were" by no means "unwrung," I marched on foot; and although such exercise suited both my tastes and habits well, still as a warning to my soldier-servant to avoid a too great frequency of the inconvenience resulting from my baggage-animals having sore backs, I always made him carry his knapsack when they were thus afflicted, but relieved him from his burden when they were sound and well. I give this hint to uninitiated young officers, as I found my plan answered completely. Sore backs were always engendered from neglect in the man who loaded the mules, by omitting to double the horse-cloths and blankets under the saddles and pack-saddles, so as to prevent local pressure on their withers or loins. When the soldier-servant finds that he relieves his own back by taking care of those of his master's animals, fewer raws are established in every way.

We now for the tenth time passed the Coa. Our line of march led us along the frontiers of Portugal and Spain, by the back of the Serra d'Estrella through the towns and villages of Aldea da Ponte, Sabugal, Castelhero, Carea, Elpendrinha Lardoso, Castello Branco, Atalaya, passing the Tagus at Villa Velha, and so on to Niza, Gavião, and Abrantes, a distance of 150 miles. I had some capital partridge-shooting on our line of march; and, much to the disgust of our chief of brigade, on one occasion I shot a fox, I was threatened, for so unsportsmanlike an act, by our sport-loving Brigadier Sir H. C, never to be allowed leave of absence, which he jokingly said he could not find it in his conscience to grant to the author of so atrocious a proceeding. As I never, however, asked for a day's leave from my duties during the three years and a half I served in the Peninsula, his observation mattered little, had it been even made in earnest.

As we arrived at each place of halt, I used to take my gun and an excellent English setter, my companion, and generally furnished my table, and that of a comrade or two, with pleasanter provision than was issued out by the commissary of his most gracious Majesty King George the Third, God bless him! We halted eleven days at Abrantes, which is a good town. Here we fitted our men's clothing, and prepared ourselves for our prospective operations in procuring such necessaries as we conceived we might want. For the first time since my arrival with the army I found myself in possession of a small bell-tent, sent out to me from England by my friends. Our poor men had no such essentials till the following year.

Two days after reaching Abrantes, my friend Gurwood of the 52nd dined with me, on his way through to embark at Lisbon for England. I remember our having a very merry party; he was full of the well-deserved honours he had gained, and we, in high spirits and health, were animated with the hope to obtain the like should the opportunity be offered us. The night dwindled into the little hours of morning ere we parted, some of us never to meet our gallant friend again,—amongst them, Harvey[10] and Burgess of the Coldstream, who fell later in this campaign, the last while heading a storming party, thus emulating his former brother officer of the 52nd in all but his success, poor fellow!

In addition to commanding my company, I now had imposed upon me the duties of Adjutant, as the officer holding that office in my corps had proceeded on leave to Lisbon. My time was pretty well occupied therefore, and sometimes not agreeably. Our Chief of battalion was by no means blessed with too strong a head, or too soft a temper; he certainly had the merit

---

10. Son of the late Admiral Sir Eliab Harvey.

sometimes to acknowledge himself in the wrong, though that wrong became tiresome, as more frequent in its recurrence than his acknowledgement of it.

He was a gallant, thick-headed man; and if the former quality palliates the latter, and charity covers a multitude of sins, still vulgar violence certainly modifies a multitude of virtues. He was a remarkable contrast to those who had preceded and succeeded him in command; the latter of whom, almost without exception, rose to well-earned honours and distinctions. We obeyed orders however, and indemnified ourselves by laughing at what could not be avoided.

A friend of mine in another corps used to say, that he flattered himself in the course of his military life he had been commanded by the greatest number of fools in the service, but that on this occasion we certainly seemed to have appropriated to ourselves one whom he quite longed to add to the list of his experiences. If men in command will but reflect that "more flies are caught with a spoonful of honey than a barrel of vinegar," and that, with power accorded them, tact and management may lead to willing instead of unwilling obedience, any person of moderate intellect will prefer that line which is surest, best, and easiest of accomplishment, to that which is the opposite.

When officers from home came out to us, we found them too frequently impregnated with all the punctilios enforced by the Horse Guards' clock; with ideas redolent of hair-powder and blank cartridge; stiff in stocks, starched in frills, with Dundas's eighteen manoeuvres or commandments. All this had to be changed. A normal school for real soldiers was undergoing the process of formation; the newcomers at first thought they had tumbled amongst a strange, loose set of half-wild men, little in accordance with their preconceived opinions. At length they began to discover how the art was carried on, and found that they had much to unlearn, as well as much to acquire, before they could make themselves useful.

Materials for the contemplated siege of Badajoz were now collecting, and passing through Abrantes towards the neighbourhood of their destined use. Scarcity of these, and inefficient transport, was, as usual, the prevailing difficulty to be fought against. In spite of all that had been done, and pointed out, and recommended by our chief, still our ministers at home, although they continued the war, starved it. Neither money nor necessaries were forthcoming when wanted; the means were always inadequate to the end. Sufficiency of artillery could not be transported from Ciudad to Badajoz; a supply of guns, of the necessary calibre of twenty-four pounders, could not be obtained at Lisbon.

Admiral Berkeley, when applied to, said he had not the means to afford them. Local preparations had been silently proceeding at Elvas, but still dearth of stores, and tools, and guns, and shot existed, attributable to the want of conduct of our Government at home, in civil as well as military matters, towards this army during the greater part of the Peninsular war.

I beg to refer on these points not only to the Duke of Wellington's own despatches on the subject, but also to his brother the Marquis Wellesley's statements concerning the administration of that day. He says, "They were timid without prudence, narrow without energy, profuse without the fruits of expenditure, and slow without the benefits of caution;"in spite of all which, our chief fairly dragged these "timid, doubting, vacillating ministers through the sloughs of their mediocrity at the wheels of his triumphal car."

If these men, with whom he was in constant counsel, heeded not his warning voice, others, both in and out of Parliament, not having similar advantages, might be excused for doubting of a success they had no means of testing or comprehending. The precedents before their eyes, and their reminiscences of military expeditions, both in conception and execution, were taken from Holland, Walcheren, and Buenos Ayres, and those there commanding. The puissant at home thought with Shakespeare, that:

*reputation is an idle and most false imposition, oft got without merit.*

From beginning to end our chiefs merits were disputed, his opinions contradicted, and his demands neglected. These people could not comprehend that one man should do a deed that none other but himself could have accomplished. A French author, Monsieur Maurel, says,

*Mais personne, ni amis, ni ennemis, personne ne soupçonnait alors ce que c'était que Wellington; l'Angleterre elle-même ne l'a connu que très-tard, et il y a une portion considérable du peuple Anglais qui ne sait pas bien au juste tout ce qu'il lui doit.*

And again, another Frenchman, not very easily suspected of partialities to England or the English, Monsieur Thiers, writes:—

There is no use in denying it—every circumstance considered, the Duke of Wellington was the greatest general whom the late wars have offered for human contemplation; his mind was so equally poised, notwithstanding the vivacity of his genius, that he was always ready, and equally prompt, on every occasion: he united the powerful combination of Napoleon to the steady judgement of Moreau. Each of these mighty captains was, perhaps, in some degree superior to Wellington in his peculiar walk.

Napoleon may have had more rapidity of view and plan upon the battlefield, and could suddenly change his whole line of battle, as at Marengo. Moreau everywhere understood better the management of a retreating army before an exulting enemy. But the exquisite apprehension and intelligence of Arthur Wellesley served him instead of both, and took at once the conduct and the measures that the occasion required.

Many of our military (*French!*) men have contested his genius, but no man can deny him the most equable judgement that was ever met with in a great soldier. It is this admirable judgement, this discerning wisdom of the mind, which has misled Europe as to his genius. Men do not expect to see in the same person the active and the passive spirit equally great; nor does nature usually bestow such opposite gifts on the same person.

In Napoleon, a steady judgement and an endurance of calamity were not the concomitants of his impulsive genius and tremendous activity; while Moreau had all his passive greatness. But the Duke of Wellington has united the two qualities. Nay, more: the noble army he had so long commanded had gradually learnt to partake of the character of their leader. No soldiers in the world but the English could have stood those successive charges, and that murderous artillery, which they so bravely bore at Waterloo.

## CHAPTER 10

# Operations Against Badajos

Having completed the fitting of our men's clothing, and furnished ourselves with what we could get as necessary for hard marching and active service, on the 3rd of March we once more moved on Elvas by Gavião, Garfete, Flores de Rosa, Alta do Chão, to Fronteira, which we reached on the 7th. Here we again halted for a few days. All the troops were now concentrating towards Badajoz, preparatory to the siege. Lord Wellington still remained at Frenada in the north, from whence he wrote to Lord Liverpool as follows:—

All my arrangements preparatory to the attack of Badajoz are in train, and, I believe, getting on well. Some of the troops have marched for the Alemtejo, and others will follow soon, and I intend to go myself the last, as I know that my removal from one part of the country to the other will be the signal for the enemy, that the part to which I am going is to be the scene of active operations.

In accordance with these views, Lord Wellington remained on the banks of the Coa, and did not arrive at Elvas till the 11th of March. We were for the moment well lodged in Fronteira, which was a capital village, in distance four leagues from the good town of Estremoz, and therefore in a convenient and comfortable neighbourhood.

The Alemtejo in general, and this part of it in particular, had suffered less from the ravages of war than most other provinces of Portugal. The climate is milder and the soil more fertile than on the rugged northern frontier of the kingdom. Here we were informed that Hill's corps had moved on to Merida and Talavera Real. The enemy had much strengthened Badajoz, by repairing the ramparts, remounting guns, adding to the outworks, and forming mines. The garrison consisted of 4000 French and 1000 German troops, with 150 cavalry. Phillipon, a general of engineers and a clever man, was in command. He had already been a prisoner in England, but had escaped by breaking his parole; and, strange to say, was again opposed to us as governor of this fortress.

Pontoons were now being brought up to form a bridge over the Guadiana. We were all very sanguine as to the result. If not interrupted by Marmont's or Soult's armies, we had little doubt of success. Two ways alone offered, to evade interruption: one was to take the place before the enemy could collect their forces to annoy us; the other was to cover the siege by corps in advance, fight a general action, and disable them from further interference with our occupations. The season was favourable, the weather fine, and not too hot. We still had the equinoctial rains to look forward to,—rather cooling torrents to encounter before the broiling heats of a Peninsular summer set in. Lord Wellington writes from Elvas as follows[1]:—

> I had intended to commence the operations against Badajoz between the 6th and 7th of March, and all my arrangements were made accordingly; but, because the large and rich town of Evora, which has suffered in no manner by the war, would supply no carriages, I could not commence till the 17th. At this moment the powder for the siege, and much of the shot, and many of the engineers' stores, are not arrived at Elvas, and we are obliged to consume the stores of that garrison. I am destroying the equipments of the army in transporting the stores from Elvas to the ground of the siege, because no assistance is given by the

---

1. See *Despatches to Lord Liverpool.*

country, or assistance quite inadequate to the demand and wants of the service, etc.

I cannot however avoid taking the opportunity of calling the attention of your Lordship and of his Majesty's Government to the neglect of the Portuguese authorities to furnish the means of transport necessary for the success of this or any other operation.

My own anxiety, and the detail into which I am obliged to enter, in order to find resources to overcome difficulties which occur at every moment, I put out of the question, although I believe no officer at the head of an army was ever so hampered, and it is desirable that the attention of one in that situation should be turned to other objects. But the serious inconveniences to which the troops are exposed, and the difficulties and risks which attend the execution of all services for want of means of transport, become of such magnitude that no officer can venture to be responsible for them; and I hope that his Majesty's Government will exert their influence with the Prince Regent of Portugal, to order the local Government not only to frame a law which shall have for its object the equipment of the armies in such a manner as to enable them to defend the country, but to carry that law into execution, so that the people of the country shall understand that they must comply with its provisions.

Why our Government, furnishing as they did an army, together with the money and munitions of war, in defence of Portugal, did not, previous to this advanced period of our operations, diplomatically and effectively stipulate for the means to carry that war on, especially as all that was required of the people was paid for by us, was best known to our ministers at home, but was perfectly unaccountable to anybody else. Inadequate as were our supplies, we had not the effective means of moving what we had. Lord Wellington was constantly at the last stretch of his ingenuity to provide what was wanting, or procure the necessary means towards the end. He was constantly acquainting our Government at home of this fact, with but slight or no result. On one occasion he remonstrated with them in the following words:—

> It is the duty of the King's Ministers to provide supplies for the service, and not to undertake a service for which they cannot provide adequate supplies of money and every other requisite.

These worse than errors of our Government at home were overcome by the extraordinary energy and determination of the great man who commanded; but, as the vice of ill supporting and attempting to control military men in what concerns their own profession seems inherent in our English Government, it may be as well to observe that the want of a cordial support and a love of dictation by unprofessional authorities in the face of all experience can have but one result, and that a mischievous one[2].

A soldier is bound to obey, and must do so; but that is no reason why the commander of an army should be expected to accomplish objects without being afforded the means required; or that his views, actions, and movements should be thwarted or overborne by the ideas of non-professional and irresponsible governors or ministers. However salutary and necessary their views may be in ordinary times, they have a most pernicious effect in war, or under circumstances which require rapidity of decision and unhampered energy. *In the life of nations, as in that of individuals, there are moments which decide their fate for years. To use that moment is success, to lose it is ruin.* In England the undue influence and love of interference by civilian ministers with the strategical operations of a military commander is the very worst species of Aulic Council.

---

2. I much fear it will be found that the late universally-regretted General Godwin experienced in no slight degree the disadvantages of this system in the Burmese war. Sir Charles Napier says, in his *Defects of the Indian Government*. "Of fourteen commanders-in-chief in India, since the year 1792, ten have resigned before their term (of service) was out; and of those who did not, two were governors-general; the others, but two, held their commands to the last, 'suffering all things.'"

The Austrian machine, detrimental as it was to freedom of movement, was at least composed of military men, who might be supposed to comprehend what they dictated; but this illegitimate control with us happens to be the very reverse with regard to any professional knowledge, and is likely therefore to prove, if possible, still more calamitous. England's great chief often said, "Never make a little war;" it would be still better, if possible, to never make any; but when you do, be in earnest. Let your supply be ample in men, and not niggardly in quantity and efficiency of material; well weigh the merits of him who is appointed to the critical post of commander, but, when chosen, support him effectively, grant him full confidence, then throw on him, if you will, all the responsibility of his free action[3].

Generally speaking, in the men of our army, there was to be found much more audacity of personal than of moral courage, caused probably by the early habit of submission to discipline, and a too great deference for the opinions of those above them, interfering with the feeling of self-reliance. The great and remarkable exception was Lord Wellington himself; and he felt this advantage so strongly, that, whatever official rebuke he found it necessary to inflict on individuals, for want of judgement in acting or not acting for themselves, he always gave those under him the aid of his public support, by which he encouraged a feeling that he himself so eminently possessed. He is a bad workman who finds fault with his tools; correcting, but also upholding, men placed in highly difficult positions, is the best of all possible ways of being well served.

---

3. A similar misunderstanding between the Government at home and the commander abroad, or rather a similar incapacity in the home Government, occurred in the great war of Hannibal with Borne. After the annihilation of the Roman army at Cannæ, the Carthaginian general sent envoys to Carthage, to demand fresh supplies of men and money, and, above all, a well-appointed battering train, in order to enable him, on the opening of the next year's campaign, to attack Rome itself. The reply of the Anti-Barcha party, as represented by its mouthpiece Hanno, was that since Hannibal had, according to his own account, achieved such successes in the field, he must be fully competent to provide himself henceforward both with the sinews and the engines of war. Hannibal was consequently disabled, by this unreasonable parsimony, from following up his movements in the field, and Rome was saved.

On the 14th, at half an hour's warning, we left Fronteira, and marched by Alta do Chão to Elvas, were we bivouacked between Port la Lippe and that town. With the exception of the Fifth Division, still on the Coa, and Hill's corps in advance in Spain, all our legions were assembled here preparatory to our destined operations against Badajoz. Lord Wellington had already arrived. I was frequently asked to dine at head-quarters. I have a lively remembrance on this occasion of passing a pleasant evening in one of the best houses the town of Elvas afforded.

The assembled party amounted to some eighteen, among whom were the authorities of the town, some ladies, two commanding officers of the regiments of the Guards, other younger and lively characters belonging to Lord Wellington's personal staff and the corps *en bivouac* in the city's neighbourhood. Lord Wellington was in high spirits, and very attentive to two pretty Portuguese young ladies, whose names I heard, but have forgotten, although at the time I was introduced to them. With great liveliness they possessed good manners, spoke French well, and of course formed the centre of attraction.

During dinner there was a man, to what corps belonging has escaped my memory, whose appetite exceeded everything but our astonishment at it, and his own surprise at finding himself surrounded by so many dainties. Certainly, in those days of scarcity, an invitation to a decent dinner was well worthy of attention. The commissaries and some few of the generals, according to their capabilities, might occasionally indulge their hospitality. Lord Wellington, although personally moderate in all his habits, still, as circumstances permitted, kept the best table going, as he was in possession of a good French cook and a *maître d'hôtel*.

The attention of the latter, as well as our own, was excited in no ordinary degree by the development of the unaccustomed guest's powers. His youthful passion for pastry made *pâté* after *pâté* disappear, for to the rapidity of a conjurer he added the swallow of a cormorant. He by no means confined himself to such light material however, and shortly proved that he was not purely farinaceous, by turning his abilities to more substantial fare with equally strong marks of a monopolizing spirit. Like the camel at the spring in the desert, he seemed determined to lay in a stock which should bear him harmless against all coming privation.

After having unconsciously occasioned us considerable amusement, in which our great chief participated with as much zest as the youngest amongst us, and that mirth and wine had sufficiently circulated, we all rose together with the ladies from table, and retired to the drawing-room. In the course of the evening the two young ladies, under the sanction of their respectable bundle of a maternity, gratified Lord Wellington's taste for music by singing many pretty airs, amongst which a duet so forcibly struck me as to stamp the air in my memory even to this day. The words ran thus:—

*Lindos olhos matadores*
*Tem a gentil bella Arminda,*
*Tem a gentil bella Arminda.*
*Alvos dentes, boca linda.*
*Gosto della mas porem*
*Tenho medo dos amores;*
*São crueis, não pagão bem,*
*São crueis, não pagão bem.*

The charms of song and the bright eyes of those who sang shed their soft influence on us. A gallant troubadour, Colonel Fermor of the Guards, was so inspired as to indulge the ladies *en revanche* with several French romances. Thus concluded an agreeable evening, which carried with it some humanizing remembrances; and as we returned to our Orson-like life in the fields, we thought with regret of these pleasant hours that had but too speedily passed.

On the 15th, at about a league from Elvas, a pontoon bridge had been laid over the Guadiana, and by daybreak on the following morning we were on foot again. The successful opening of a campaign always acts favourably on the spirits of a soldiery; and now Lord Wellington was about to fulfil his promise previously made to Lord Liverpool, that "if we took Ciudad Rodrigo we should make a fine campaign in the spring."

In furtherance of this assurance we crossed the Guadiana on the 16th of March, 1812, to commence movements and operations which lasted, without interruption, until the middle of the November following. On the 16th Badajoz was invested by Marshal Beresford, who crossed the river, and drove in the enemy's outposts. The Third, Fourth, and Light Divisions, and a brigade of Hamilton's Portuguese, about 15,000 men, were destined for the attack of the fortress.

The First, Sixth, and Seventh Divisions, and two brigades of cavalry, formed a corps under our divisional chief, Sir Thomas Graham, and our movements were directed by Valverde and Santa Martha upon Llerena; Hill moved by Merida upon Almendralejos. These corps acted as a covering army to protect the operations of the siege, and amounted to 30,000. The Fifth Division was on the march from Beira; and the whole army consisted of about 51,000 sabres and bayonets, of which 20,000 were Portuguese[4]. Soult's army at this time was between Seville and Cadiz, and some movable columns of Drouet's and Daricau's, of about 5000 men each, at Villa Franca and near Medellin.

Before entering further into notice of movements necessarily connected with my anecdotical journal, I may mention that Lord Wellington, in taking the field, thought proper to inaugurate the event by giving a grand *fête* to Field-Marshal Beresford and his staff, a cordial to his friends, as an introduction to the more inimical operation of the siege of Badajoz,—thus following the soldier's motto,

*Let us be merry today, for tomorrow we die*[5].

Near Badajoz there was no house or building within half a mile of the spot selected for Lord Wellington's head-quarter camp. It was a bleak and barren place enough, the only advantage being that, although within range, it was concealed by some rising ground from the fire of the fortress. During the

---

4. See *Napier*.

siege however two or three shells did fall amongst these canvas residences. The tents for the use of the two Headquarter Staffs of the British and Portuguese armies were brought from Elvas that morning; they arrived at their destination at nine o'clock; the ground was marked out, the tents erected, the kitchens made, a substantial oven built by transporting materials from the stone wall of a vineyard half a mile off, mortar was concocted, wood for fuel collected, and everything accomplished before one o'clock, at which time that man of celebrity the chef or head cook, reached his scene of glory.

Surrounded and within range of all the warlike implements of destruction, this greater than Vatel "*a parfaitement conservé son sang-froid dans ses entrées.*" At half-past two, the elements on which his art depended arrived on foot. The bullocks, poor things! little thought of the uses to which they were walking, or that their respectable parts (although their forms partook of the greyhound cut) would be so precipitately transubstantiated into joints, gravy, and gelatinous substances. They however were killed, skinned, and cut up; and by six o'clock were served up to a company of distinguished men in as many savoury shapes as any party of guests in Grosvenor-square ever sat down to dawdle over,—the difference being that air and exercise, and a too great absence of plenty, occasioned a somewhat different appreciation of the indulgence, and a keener sense of the value of things.

Dryden's recommendation of

*Take the goods the gods provide thee*

was then turned from a poetical to a practical fact, leaving "lovely Thais" out of the question, unfortunately because nobody had much time to attend to her, poor lady! It may be seen, from the sudden preparations and rapid accomplishment of this banquet, that in pleasure, as well as business, the grass was never allowed to grow under our feet. Without half the ceremony I

---

5. Lieutenant-General Lord Keane, when commander-in-chief at Jamaica, had these words written over his dining-room door, —I suppose, in compliment to the yellow fever.

have alluded to, and with the slightest possible disguise by cookery, I have often seen a lean, well-travelled bullock killed and eaten in half an hour, his hide and horns alone remaining in demonstration of what he once had been.

Having passed the pontoon bridge over the Guadiana, we entered on immense plains of unwholesome and malaria-like appearance, producing coarse grass and great quantities of the wild garlic. We followed no road. The First, Sixth, and Seventh Divisions, and two brigades of cavalry, marched in contiguous columns over this wide and tiresome expanse of level. Neither tree nor hill was to be seen. No living thing was visible except innumerable hares, which sprang up amidst our columns. The men's shouts drove them like shuttlecocks from one to the other, till, bewildered by noise, and surrounded by foes, followed by every yelping cur, galloped after by every officer they approached, they fell a sacrifice in endeavouring to force their way through our ranks.

In their endeavours to escape they were almost all killed, and afforded capital sport to the many, and no slight profit to the few. Between forty and fifty hares graced the bivouac fires of our camp this day. The weather in the morning was mild and pleasant, though dark and lowering, but in the evening it became cold and rainy. We bivouacked this night near Valverde, a village in a decent state of preservation.

This night, for the first time, I felt the genial comfort attached to the proprietorship of a tent. I had thus suddenly become *le petit propriétaire* in reality, and indulged in the pride of possession: the more so as it was the first tenement of any kind that ever really belonged to me, and I hastened to show a proper sense of the claims of hospitality by sharing it with a tentless comrade. Ensconced beneath its cover this tempestuous night, we smoked our cigars, and listened in contemptuous security to the pattering rain driven by the wild wind against its sides.

The disagreeable remembrance of being frequently out on such a night as this, peculiarly recommended to us the advantage of being within. Those happy young fellows lately at Chobham camp had a sufficiency of bad weather probably to make them estimate at a guess the disadvantage of being on the wrong side of canvas, and might possibly have presented to their minds a comparison between the inside seat of a first-class railway carriage and the outside one on a donkey in a storm. It was with grateful feelings towards those kind friends who had sent me this defence against weather, that we drank to them with the soldier's toast,

*Here's a health to all absent friends, God bless them.*

They, alas! with many others, are gone, and can no more read the passing record of my gratitude.

On the 17th the Third and Fourth and Light Divisions broke ground before Badajoz; but as our *corps d'armée,* under Graham, advanced towards the south, we knew little and heard nothing in detail of the operations in our rear. We had an enemy in front who was to occupy our attention, and we wished, in return, to occupy his, by preventing his dwelling too pertinaciously on the operations of the siege that we were destined to mask. In the meantime we had to feel for the enemy's movable columns, which we knew to be in our neighbourhood, and consequently outposts, patrols, and piquets were in plenty. We moved on Santa Martha; a small force belonging to Soult's corps retired as we advanced. It was reported that Marmont was at Talavera de la Reyna.

We continued our movements by La Para to Zafra, an excellent town, which the enemy had left but a few hours before we entered it. The weather was so bad and the Spanish towns so good, that we left off bivouacking and were sheltered in most agreeable and capital quarters. We were delighted with this part of Spain, and with the comparatively clean, good houses,—their well whitewashed exteriors indented by substantial doors and iron-grated windows, from whence peeped forth the dark *houri* eyes of the Spanish women,—the good-nature and lively manners of these people, their guitars, their song and dance.

Though too short our stay, Zafra was to us a pleasant place;

in comparison to the rough life we led, quite an oasis in the desert. Short of labouring on the land, we had become by living in it the purest of all possible species of agriculturists, for we sojourned entirely in the fields, woods, bogs, and mountains. The roofs which were destined to shelter us in Portugal were widely different and greatly inferior to those offered us in Spain, and resembled more, with due deference to Hibernian proprietors, an Irish hovel than a human habitation.

In Spain, although not quit of those hopping vampires ,the fleas, always to be found in southern climates, the people, the towns, and houses stood us in compensation. Besides, after a man had been some time on service in these countries, his mental as well as his bodily feelings became hardened: the latter by degrees partook of the rhinoceros, and both at length defied the petty stings of fortune and of vermin. Our taste for Spanish towns increased with experience; being already on the road to Seville, we hoped, before we finished our promenade, to reach the cities of the south so much lauded in the native tongue.

*Quien no ha visto Sevilla,*
*No ha visto maravilla;*
*Quilon no ha vieto Granada,*
*No ha visto nada.*

Eighteen more years from this period were to elapse before I was to tread the streets and visit the Alcazar of Seville, and enjoy the scenes and the climate of the Vega of Granada, with all the grandeur of its overhanging Sierra de Nevada, and the beautiful remains of its Morescan palaces. The people of this part of Spain,—the middle and lower order, for of the high classes we saw little, and what we did see was by no means prepossessing,—are a remarkably handsome, fine-looking race, occasionally betraying a tinge of the Saracen blood, mixed with the *sangre azul,* which spoke in palliation of the Valencian proverb:—

*Buen cielo, buen tierra,*
*Mai entre tierra y cielo*[6].

6. Which may be translated thus:—*Fair sky, fair land; All between, nothing grand.*

Still there was amongst them an assimilation in tastes to their not far distant neighbours the Italians, and the *dolce far niente* seemed to prevail. When roused to energy they may be induced to act, but, with pompous promises and grandiloquent phrases, postponement and the fear of troubling their lazy intellects predominated. It was always *mañana,* but never today, with them. To put off everything, seemed looked upon as the acme of all that was clever; and never to do that which they could persuade another to do for them, was the perfection of dexterity. Their whole mind, in short, seemed bent upon doing nothing, and—they did it. At the same time there is no want of quickness or intelligence in them. When imperative interest or passion urges, they display all the readiness of resource and acuteness so truthfully depicted in the character of Figaro.

On occasion of the movements of some of the enemy's flying columns employed against the Spanish guerrillas, as our detective police might be against pickpockets, the French marched on a Spanish town to punish it for some real or pretended grievance. The people fled, as, innocent or guilty, they well knew the result would be disastrous. They left their houses in the night, or, as our sergeant-major, a man of eloquence, used to say, they "surreptitiously and promiscuously took their departure."

Of all the inhabitants, two young girls, of considerable personal attractions, alone remained, in a house belonging to one of the authorities of the town. Their alarm at such a visit of vengeance may be conceived. They well knew that their good looks were their least defensive quality; *for beauty provoketh thieves sooner than gold.* No means of escape presenting itself, the elder directed the younger to retire to her bed, which could scarcely be considered the safest place in the house.

Militarily, it seemed a false position to assume for a weak garrison intending a resolute defence, but what will address and good tactic not accomplish? She painted her sister's face a ghastly white, and gave to the apartment all the air of a sick room. These preparations had scarcely been completed when the enemy, arriving from different directions, finding nothing in kitchen or cellar, set about exploring the other rooms. On entering the supposed invalid's apartment, the nursing sister, in the deepest apparent affliction, covering her face with a handkerchief, broke out into loud lamentations—"*Madre de Dios! la pobrecica tiene una calentura contagiosa—la peste*[7]"

The French rushed out instantaneously, vacating the quarter even more promptly than they had entered it, echoing the cry as they went—"*La peste! la peste! le diable emporte la peste!*" The obtrusive visit of their would-be conquerors was thus disposed of by these ready-witted beauties.

It must be confessed, however, that to the female portion of the community *Messieurs les Français* generally made themselves very acceptable; and although the Spanish women complained of them, saying that "*Los ladrones Franceses* have eaten all our Andalucian bulls, killed our poultry, and knocked from their niches every emblem of the Virgin," still many of them were sufficiently imbued with the attributes of Christian charity to return good for evil, and not to allow their patriotic prejudices to overcome their personal feelings. In all characters that a Frenchman may be called upon to enact, he is always proverbially insinuating, gay, and agreeable; and the Spanish women, if there be truth in our experience, seemed well disposed to act up to their national proverb, of—

> *Todo el mundo es un bolero,*
> *El que no bayla es un tonto*[8].

It was with great regret that on the 21st we left Zafra to occupy Fuentes del Meistro, where however we still found good cantonments,—the more acceptable as the weather continued very bad. Although this town was fourteen leagues from Badajoz, we could distinctly hear the cannonade, as its deep, unfriendly sound came undulating through the air. We here heard that the enemy had made a sortie, in which they lost some men; that Colonel Fletcher, our chief engineer, had been wounded, and

---

7. Mother of our Lord! the poor little thing has a contagious fever—the plague.
8. *All the world is a ball, and he is a fool who does not dance..*

that Captain Cuthbert, Picton's *aide-de-camp*, had been killed; that some of our batteries were to have opened on this day, and that a breach might be expected to be rendered practicable in about ten days.

With regard to our covering corps, the Seventh Division was at Villa Franca, some of our cavalry at Zafra, and the rest at Llerena and its environs. Marmont, report said, was still at Talavera de la Reyna with 36,000 men (which however was doubtful); Suchet at Valencia. Soult was occupied in collecting his forces, some 20,000, at Seville and its neighbourhood; and 10,000 more of the enemy were at this time at or near Medellin. We were all full of conjecture. Many seemed to think that a general action would shortly ensue. I remember differing with some of my comrades on this point. I thought that our foes were not likely to attack us unless they could hope to raise the siege, and this they could not do unless they brought down on us their whole force.

The distance between their different corps prohibited a combination within a probable time to save the fortress. Without such a hope, it was useless and not to their advantage to fight, as there was nothing to fight for. Marmont was said to display no inclination to act in conjunction with Soult, but we subsequently discovered, from intercepted despatches, that the Emperor's orders directed him to operate in the north and on the banks of the Coa, threatening an irruption into the province of Beira in Portugal.

On further information we found that the delay occasioned by the bad weather, want of *matériel,* and inefficiency of transport had still further postponed the opening of our batteries against Badajoz. At the same time Lord Wellington himself said, we were not by 20,000 men so strong on the left bank of the Guadiana as we ought to be.

We were uncertain also of Drouet's whereabouts; he was believed to be in the neighbourhood of Don Benito, with a view to protect the junction of Foy by the bridge of Medellin. Lord Wellington's intention was to move our right divisions and the cavalry to Zalamea and Quintana, at the same time that our left division from Almendralejos should reach Oliva, and Hill's corps Medellin, and thus force back the enemy from their best communications across the Guadiana with Soult, and by thus intercepting them create delay in their conjunctive movements. But we could not hope to maintain this position long, as Soult could move from the south on our right flank, or, if he chose, on our rear. To gain Badajoz, therefore, we were once more fighting against time, as we did at Ciudad Rodrigo. The difference was, that here the task was tougher; the place from natural position as well as art being stronger, its garrison more numerous, and its governor more able.

At Fuentes del Meistro, having marched on foot from the northern frontier of Spain, a distance of between three and four hundred miles, I here purchased another mule, although our adjutant, whose duties devolved upon me, had left me his stud during his absence. It was fortunate I did so, as our movements now became much more rapid and harassing. A sudden thought struck the commander of our *corps d'armée;* and on the 25th, without baggage, and at the shortest possible notice, we left Fuentes del Meistro at seven a.m. and proceeded two leagues towards Los Santos, where, having halted for a few minutes only outside the town, we continued our march four leagues further, and reached Bien Venide at five p.m., having accomplished, in ten hours' march, with scarcely a check, six *leguas grandillones*, a distance most uncertain, except as to its being a short one.

The country was a dead open flat, devoid of trees, and with only occasional culture. We established our bivouac beside a small stream, in some low undulating ground, concealed under a gentle slope, and were ordered to consider ourselves *au secret*.

The day had been hot, the march rapid and harassing, and some rest was requisite. Evening closed in; the moon rose and seemed to look down in bright contempt on our barren hiding-place. Our divisions were all assembled here, but at ten at night we were on foot again, directing our march on the town of Llerena. We now discovered that this secret and forced march was for the purpose of surprising a small flying column of the enemy, consisting of some 2600 men belonging to Drouet's corps.

The operation was an attempted imitation of the Arroyo de Molinos affair, so cleverly executed by Hill in the previous campaign of 1811, 11,000 infantry, 2000 cavalry, and twenty-four pieces of artillery, were formed in contiguous columns; the First, Sixth, and Seventh Divisions in one body, the two brigades of cavalry on our left, and the twenty-four guns in our front, with some light infantry in advance.

Thus massed we moved in close order during the rest of the night. This formation forbade our availing ourselves of the road further than as a line of direction across the country we were traversing. Previous to our leaving our bivouac at Bien Venide, we heard that those we were about to seek were safely in their quarters at Llerena, in perfect ignorance of our stealthy, tiger-like approach. They were sleeping probably, and little dreaming of our intended visit to them at such an unfashionably early hour.

Unluckily, no movement of any part of our force on the enemy's flanks, to intercept their retreat, seemed to have been in contemplation, and we moved altogether in a straight line, and in one lump. We had also to take on trust the chance of the prudence and loyalty of the Spanish peasants to their own cause. As they might give information of our approach, we took the precaution of allowing none that we knew of, or could stop, to proceed in the direction of Llerena. In an open country, devoid of hill or wood, it requires, rather more address to conceal a body of some 13,000 men, in movement on its surface, than for a gentleman of the thimble-rig profession to hide his pea on the downs and heaths of Ascot or of Epsom.

The moon had set,—the night, though starlight, was dark; we marched in close formation and in strict silence, but still a large body moving over the flat face of mother earth might be detected, and the clink of cavalry sabres, the roll of the wheel-of guns, the tramp of horses, and the heavy sounding tread of 13,000 warriors might be wafted through the still night air to a distance, and attract the attentive ears set on watch to ward the approach of coming danger. A dog's bark, a bird's flight, or a hare's course, would create suspicion that some disturbing influence was on foot, and would put on the alert those well versed in outpost duty and war's alarms, thereby betraying the movements of our column.

On and on we went, in wearisome darkness and in seemingly interminable space; half-asleep and stumbling, our men blundered against each other, then again resumed their order, giving vent to some grumbling exclamation of discontent. The night was far spent, but before daylight had dawned we all at once were aroused from our monotonous heavy trudge by coming upon a cavalry patrol, despatched by the enemy from one of their neighbouring outposts to reconnoitre. They instantly fired on us and galloped off.

Had our movements been kept secret till now this rencontre must have effectively revealed them. The *contretemps* unfortunately did not end here, in consequence of all our divisions having been injudiciously ordered to load. When we came upon the enemy, the Sixth Division had on the march gained slightly in advance of the rest, and the Seventh, on receiving the fire of the French patrol, were tempted to return it, and by so doing fired into the Sixth, as the flashes of the enemy's carbines came from that direction.

Fortunately, the officers of this last column restrained their men from returning the untoward salute, or, in the surrounding darkness, we should all have been fighting one another. As it was, a surgeon, a paymaster, and six men were killed and wounded; and thus, in the most critical moment of an intended surprise, we much surprised ourselves by firing on our own people instead of the enemy, to whom, by all this noise, we gave undoubted notice of our approach. It may be imagined that some excitement ensued.

The columns were now closed up, the officers instantaneously dismounted and fell into their ranks, leaving their horses to shift for themselves. S———, who commanded the company next to mine, did not at all approve of quitting a steed he "ne'er might see again." I luckily found a little drummer, whom, in an unauthorized manner, I pressed into my service, consigning my Rosinante to his charge. My mind, being made easy on that score, was turned in anxious expectation to what would next follow.

We still moved forward, marching over some of the bodies that the Seventh Division had slain; at length, at daybreak, we arrived within a short distance of the town of Llerena; and as objects became more visible, we discovered our enemy on the other side of it, quietly marching away, leaving us to our reflections. A parting shot or two from our guns, by way of acquainting them with our address, was the only communication that ensued between us.

Our long march, like auld Meestress M'Sillygossip's long story, related by the late Mr. Mathews in his *At Home,* was a wearisome prolixity without a point. A forced march of nearly fifty miles had been accomplished in nineteen hours, by a body of 13,000 men, for the purpose of surprising 2600 of the enemy; but as no detached flank movements were attempted to intercept or even interrupt their retreat, they marched out of one end of the town of Llerena as we marched into the other.

Had the execution of our movements been supported by strategical combinations, the result might have been different. As it was however, we were so far successful that, by driving back on its reserve this small advance corps of Drouet, we effectually interrupted any immediate communication between him, Daricau, and Soult. The enemy exchanged some few shots with our light troops, when they went their way, and we saw no more of them.

After our fatiguing but somewhat futile attempt, we were rewarded by a twenty-four hours' halt in the good town of Llerena. Good towns being as scarce as the opportunities we had of enjoying them, this indulgence was duly appreciated by way of compensation for our disappointments.

Next day, our baggage having come up, after a refreshing rest in our excellent quarters, we moved again four leagues further to a bivouac near Marguillas. This village is situated on a plateau between the streams of the Coracha and Matachiel, at the foot and no great distance from one of the spurs, or offshoots, of the Sierra Morena, running down in this direction to the plains beneath.

Here, to our astonishment, the German Legion and our brigade remained quiet for a few days: we were in a happy state of uncertainty, although kept in constant readiness and expectation to move. The other two divisions had gone forward; the Seventh to Asuaga, and the Sixth to Berlenga on our right, in the direction of Seville, on the road leading to the south. Major-General Stopford's Brigade of infantry was pushed still further forward in the same direction, and as far as Quadalcanal.

Various reports reached us concerning the enemy, but nothing that could be depended on. The breaching batteries at Badajoz were to open on the 31st, and should the enemy intend to make an attempt to interrupt our operations, or relieve the fortress, they had not a moment to lose. Hill's corps was still in the neighbourhood of Medellin.

On the 1st of April we left Marguillas, moving in a retrograde direction on Badajoz, by Llera and Usagre to Los Santos. Here our route was changed from that of Fuentes del Meistro to La Para, then to Almandral, and thence to a bivouac in the woods in front of the position of Albuera, where, after a five days' march, all our corps, under Sir Thomas Graham, were again concentrated, ready once more to occupy the old battlefield, if rendered necessary by the enemy's advance. Of them we heard nothing, but surmised, from these movements of ours, that they were approaching.

During this march a gay and gallant young guardsman, *aide-de-camp* to Sir Rowland Hill, reached us with communications from his chief. A better informed and more agreeable companion and good soldier was not easily found. We were about the same age and standing, and our acquaintance, begun here, ripened into great intimacy in after-life, for I never gambled, borrowed, or lent him money! Lively, brave, and warm-hearted, he was, alas! reckless, thoughtless, and extravagant; would lend or give you, while he had it, all he had; but could afford to owe you, even to the Greek Kalends, any amount of cash you lent him. I fear it might be said of him that he never paid a debt, except that to nature.

His reckless gallantry lost him his life in India, where he fell, much lamented. Peace be to his manes! I loved him well, in spite of his faults, for he had many good and even great qualities. His name matters not; it was well known and distinguished in our military annals of the preceding century; his friends will recognize it but too well in reading this tribute to his memory.

In our ilex and cork-wood bivouac, *en attendant* the expected advance of Soult, our men hutted themselves. From those excellent troops, the Hanoverian Legion belonging to the division, our men learned much in this as well as many other useful arts. The Germans displayed great ingenuity in rural architecture, forming commodious turf-and-leafy dwellings half underground, small sunken snuggeries, very cleverly contrived, and adapted to the nature of their necessities.

Serving as a defence against the heats of day, the dews of night, and the rains of spring and autumn, they were rendered more or less substantial or effective, according to circumstances and the probable time of their occupation. Light and simply defensive against the elements for a night's lodging, they became more beaver-like when a longer residence was promised. The English generally improve on the invention of others, and, in following so good an example, we even constructed stables and sheds for our horses and beasts of burden.

It was always considered one of the greatest camp conveniences, and highly diplomatic, to be well with the quarter-master of the regiment, or on intimate terms with the butcher of the brigade. They were the chiefs, the masters of the ceremonies, and distributors of the delicacies of provender (such as oxtails and lumps of suet from the well-marched and hastily-killed cattle) to the numerous hungry applicants. These, on being paid for, might, as a favour, be added to the rations of the officers; "but what was this amongst so many?"

Our good old quarter-master H———— was a character,—a perfect specimen of this class. He had risen by his merit; and, by weight, rotundity, and respectability, he maintained the dignity of his position. Possessed of great matter-of-fact good sense, he was an honest, bright-faced, downright old soldier. He always had the best fire in all our bivouacs, and had become the oracle of all the ensigns. The "idle club" of the camp would frequently assemble around his merry bonfire, to hear or communicate the current news or reports of the day, yclept in Peninsular language "shaves."

Those handicraftsmen of our corps, the pioneers, were his attendants; and, under his orders, they were the cutters of wood, the shoers of horses, and dispensers of liquor, when such was received for distribution from the commissaries. The well-known sound of Knock, the cooper, singing out in his shrill, squeaky voice, "Cucks (cooks) for wine[9]!" may still tingle in the ears and rest in the memories of those who heard them in "auld lang syne;" and the joyous buzz and commotion created amongst our men by so welcome an announcement, may still be remembered.

In Soult's hasty retreat from Oporto in May, 1809, our brigade came suddenly on the enemy's rear-guard near Salamonde, and turned their retreat into a flight, taking from them baggage and all kinds of material. Two very powerful nags, one black and the other white, such as drag diligences in France, fell to the lot of that "tun of man," old H———— the quarter-master. He contrived always to keep these cattle—out of compliment to himself, I suppose—in an unusual state of rotund condition.

Unwieldy as he appeared, he was a perfect picture on horseback, for the combination was complete of the "Elephant and Castle," a goodly sign warmly greeted wherever met with. On the march he always headed the baggage of the brigade, and far,

---

9. The pioneers' duty, under the superintendence of the quartermaster-sergeant, was to distribute the liquor amongst the cooks of the different messes of the men.

far off in the winding distance might be seen his portly figure, on the milk-white steed, as unlike as possible to "Death on the pale horse!"

The distributions of camp delicacies from the above cavalier, or from Jones, the butcher, added in no small degree to eke out the rations of the separate messes and picnics of the officers. Seldom more than two of us messed together, chiefly those belonging to the same company or the one next in line to it. We found from experience that, however well masters might agree, it was difficult to get servants to do so, for which reason I preferred the picnic plan, instead of having a mess in common. Two or three would thus club their provender and dine together, each bringing his plates, knives, forks, and drinking cups. I well remember my friend B—— joined us frequently in this way. He always brought his *couvert,* as the French call it, but deuce the thing else in the shape of comestible or beverage. When rallied on the absence of these most essential contributions to a picnic, and accused of providing nothing, he would reply that we cruelly maligned him, for he always brought his knife, fork, and an excellent appetite.

At this bivouac near Albuera, and on the 6th of April, towards evening, a reinforcement of detachments from England reached our brigade, under the command of Lieutenant-Colonel B——, afterwards D. A., Adjutant-General to our division.

The rest of the draft was composed of four hundred men, together with two young ensigns, H—— and R——, belonging to our regiment. The first of these made a right good soldier, and was severely wounded later at Salamanca. He now sits in the House of Commons, and is an Irish peer. With this detachment I received an English spaniel, six shirts, and a groom-boy. We made our recruits as welcome and comfortable as we could, by offering such hospitality as the field afforded, and did our best to make them forget the luxuries of beef, porter, iced champagne, and sugar-plums.

Their round fresh English faces bore strong contrast to the copper-coloured, weather-beaten visages of our old hands. Recent news from dear England, brought by these blooming fellows, was very acceptable, and was received at all times with pleasure, whether coming in verbal, printed, or written shape.

After sunset, and the convivial hour of the evening meal had passed, most of us in time and due course retired to our tents and to rest. The night was dry, though mild and cloudy; everything was still save the customary croaking of frogs, or the low murmur of conversation at some bivouac fire; all but the sentries and camp guards had sunk to sleep; the occasional sound of a distant gun alone broke the silence; when at once, and as if from a volcano, explosions, like thunder, rent the air of night, and bounded along the surface of the earth. Salvo after salvo in continued succession reached the ear of the sleeping soldier, and roused him in his bivouac lair to the consciousness of the living struggle carried on by his not far distant comrades—

Lord Wellington was storming Badajoz.

LEONAUR

# ALSO FROM LEONAUR
## AVAILABLE IN SOFTCOVER OR HARDCOVER WITH DUST JACKET

**JOURNALS OF ROBERT ROGERS OF THE RANGERS** *by Robert Rogers*—The exploits of Rogers & the Rangers in his own words during 1755-1761 in the French & Indian War.

**GALLOPING GUNS** *by James Young*—The Experiences of an Officer of the Bengal Horse Artillery During the Second Maratha War 1804-1805.

**GORDON** *by Demetrius Charles Boulger*—The Career of Gordon of Khartoum.

**THE BATTLE OF NEW ORLEANS** *by Zachary F. Smith*—The final major engagement of the War of 1812.

**THE TWO WARS OF MRS DUBERLY** *by Frances Isabella Duberly*—An Intrepid Victorian Lady's Experience of the Crimea and Indian Mutiny.

**WITH THE GUARDS' BRIGADE DURING THE BOER WAR** *by Edward P. Lowry*—On Campaign from Bloemfontein to Koomati Poort and Back.

**THE REBELLIOUS DUCHESS** *by Paul F. S. Dermoncourt*—The Adventures of the Duchess of Berri and Her Attempt to Overthrow French Monarchy.

**MEN OF THE MUTINY** *by John Tulloch Nash & Henry Metcalfe*—Two Accounts of the Great Indian Mutiny of 1857: Fighting with the Bengal Yeomanry Cavalry & Private Metcalfe at Lucknow.

**CAMPAIGN IN THE CRIMEA** *by George Shuldham Peard*—The Recollections of an Officer of the 20th Regiment of Foot.

**WITHIN SEBASTOPOL** *by K. Hodasevich*—A Narrative of the Campaign in the Crimea, and of the Events of the Siege.

**WITH THE CAVALRY TO AFGHANISTAN** *by William Taylor*—The Experiences of a Trooper of H. M. 4th Light Dragoons During the First Afghan War.

**THE CAWNPORE MAN** *by Mowbray Thompson*—A First Hand Account of the Siege and Massacre During the Indian Mutiny By One of Four Survivors.

**BRIGADE COMMANDER: AFGHANISTAN** *by Henry Brooke*—The Journal of the Commander of the 2nd Infantry Brigade, Kandahar Field Force During the Second Afghan War.

**BANCROFT OF THE BENGAL HORSE ARTILLERY** *by N. W. Bancroft*—An Account of the First Sikh War 1845-1846.

**LEONAUR**

# ALSO FROM LEONAUR
## AVAILABLE IN SOFTCOVER OR HARDCOVER WITH DUST JACKET

**THE FALL OF THE MOGHUL EMPIRE OF HINDUSTAN** *by H. G. Keene*—By the beginning of the nineteenth century, as British and Indian armies under Lake and Wellesley dominated the scene, a little over half a century of conflict brought the Moghul Empire to its knees.

**LADY SALE'S AFGHANISTAN** *by Florentia Sale*—An Indomitable Victorian Lady's Account of the Retreat from Kabul During the First Afghan War.

**THE CAMPAIGN OF MAGENTA AND SOLFERINO 1859** *by Harold Carmichael Wylly*—The Decisive Conflict for the Unification of Italy.

**FRENCH'S CAVALRY CAMPAIGN** *by J. G. Maydon*—A Special Correspondent's View of British Army Mounted Troops During the Boer War.

**CAVALRY AT WATERLOO** *by Sir Evelyn Wood*—British Mounted Troops During the Campaign of 1815.

**THE SUBALTERN** *by George Robert Gleig*—The Experiences of an Officer of the 85th Light Infantry During the Peninsular War.

**NAPOLEON AT BAY, 1814** *by F. Loraine Petre*—The Campaigns to the Fall of the First Empire.

**NAPOLEON AND THE CAMPAIGN OF 1806** *by Colonel Vachée*—The Napoleonic Method of Organisation and Command to the Battles of Jena & Auerstädt.

**THE COMPLETE ADVENTURES IN THE CONNAUGHT RANGERS** *by William Grattan*—The 88th Regiment during the Napoleonic Wars by a Serving Officer.

**BUGLER AND OFFICER OF THE RIFLES** *by William Green & Harry Smith*—With the 95th (Rifles) during the Peninsular & Waterloo Campaigns of the Napoleonic Wars.

**NAPOLEONIC WAR STORIES** *by Sir Arthur Quiller-Couch*—Tales of soldiers, spies, battles & sieges from the Peninsular & Waterloo campaigns.

**CAPTAIN OF THE 95TH (RIFLES)** *by Jonathan Leach*—An officer of Wellington's sharpshooters during the Peninsular, South of France and Waterloo campaigns of the Napoleonic wars.

**RIFLEMAN COSTELLO** *by Edward Costello*—The adventures of a soldier of the 95th (Rifles) in the Peninsular & Waterloo Campaigns of the Napoleonic wars.

www.ingramcontent.com/pod-product-compliance
Lightning Source LLC
Chambersburg PA
CBHW032054080426
42733CB00006B/274